Youthanize

What Others are Saying...

I have deplored the shallow pseudo-Christian nature of most American youth ministry my entire adult life. The fact that so many youth have left the church is no surprise. So I'm delighted that Rob Cook has blessed the church with this book, especially as it rises from the authority of his gritty, hands-on ministry. Whether you're a teen or care about teens, Rob will tell you what you need to hear and show you what to do about it.

Peter Lundell, D.Miss., M.Div.

Author, missionary, pastor, Bible college instructor

"Go," was never a Suggestion. Rob Cook understands what it takes to follow God's Call down a path few are willing to travel. His book is a blueprint to help you navigate the Journey.

Rev. Chuck Kieffer

Pastor, The Foundry Church

Evangelism Catalyst, *North American Mission Board*

Host, *Up at Night* Radio

At first I thought, *oh another youth ministry book.* Wow, Robert Cook. You just never cease to amaze me. It was page after page and I just kept going with the out-of-the-box thinking that you shared.

I've been in ministry for 39 years. I think we pastors all have cut our teeth in youth ministry, and I thought I was innovative and clever in my efforts to reach the youth of our community. Then I read *Youthanize*.

I love how you break all the rules. As I read your book on the plane, I wanted to show it to everybody and tell them what a brilliant piece of literature this book is. It needs to be shared with everybody— in ministry and out of ministry. You show so many great ways to connect with youth and keep them coming back wanting more.

This book is a winner, brother, Thank you for letting me share and encourage you to keep going strong, because you've inspired me in my writings. God bless you Rob. —

Bob Ossler

co-author of *Triumph Over Terror: Ground Zero Chaplain*

I've never forgotten the night about seven years ago when a friend introduced me to Rob Cook and the ministry of *252 Underground*. The storefront was packed with kids—tough-looking kids I would have avoided if I met them on the street. But when Rob turned off the deafening music, they sat and listened—really listened to him. He made the Bible relevant to their needs as he spoke to heart and hard issues.

I believe *Youthanize* is a book that every Christian needs to read for as Rob says, "We are failing at reaching this generation. If we don't act now, I believe the very future of Christianity is at stake."

Marlene Bagnull, Litt.D.
Author and Conference Director

Time to put a toe-tag on some of the old youth ministry practices. After reading *Youthanize*, you won't be caught dead doing youth ministry exactly how you did before.

Tim Shoemaker
Author, Speaker, Writing Coach

Youthanize

THE DEATH OF TRADITIONAL YOUTH MINISTRY

Robert Cook

Taegais Publishing, LLC
Glenwood, Maryland

Copyright © 2017 by Robert Cook

Taegais Publishing LLC

978-1-940727-27-1 print
978-1-940727-28-8 ebook

Visit Author at http://www.robcookunderground.com

Cover Design by Ken Raney at https://kenraneyartandillustration.blogspot.com

Interior and Ebook design and formatting by EBook Listing Services at http://www.ebooklistingservices.com

Published by Taegais Publishing LLC at http://www.taegais.com

Scriptures taken from the Holy Bible, New International Version®, NIV®. Copyright © 1973, 1978, 1984, 2011 by Biblica, Inc.™ Used by permission of Zondervan. All rights reserved worldwide. www.zondervan.com The "NIV" and "New International Version" are trademarks registered in the United States Patent and Trademark Office by Biblica, Inc.™

Publisher's Cataloging-in-Publication data
Name: Cook, Robert, author.
Title: Youthanize : the death of traditional youth ministry / Robert Cook.
Description: Glenwood, MD: Taegais Publishing, LLC, 2017.
Identifiers: ISBN 978-1-940727-27-1 (pbk.) | 978-1-940727-28-8 (ebook) | LCCN 2017946163
Subjects: LCSH Church work with teenagers. | Non church-affiliated people. | Evangelistic work. | Christian youth--Religious life. | BISAC RELIGION / Christian Ministry / Youth
Classification: LCC BV4447 .C66 2017 | DDC 259--dc23

1 3 5 7 9 10 8 6 4 2
Printed in the United States of America

Table of Contents

Foreword by Bob Hostetler...............................ix

Prologue..1

Chapter 1: The Diagnosis..............................3

Chapter 2: What's In Your Tackle Box?........13

Chapter 3: Get in the Water..........................21

Chapter 4: Be a Rope Holder.........................27

Chapter 5: Equipping for Battle....................43

Chapter 6: Let's Make a Deal........................51

Chapter 7: When a Door Closes....................55

Chapter 8: Love's the Only Rule....................61

Chapter 9: A Different Kind of Animal..........67

Chapter 10: Main Street, Not Easy Street......77

Chapter 11: Better Than Drugs...............................89

Chapter 12: Building a Team................................93

Chapter 13: Lessons from the Master..........................99

Chapter 14: Prisoners of War...............................109

Chapter 15: A Working Model................................115

Chapter 16: Shooting Our Way Into Their Hearts.....125

Chapter 17: The Perfect Marriage..............................133

Chapter 18: CHIL Out...................................139

Chapter 19: Develop Leaders...............................143

Chapter 20: Don't Quit...................................147

Appendix: Sample Lessons.............................151

Excerpt: Regener8...................................165

Excerpt: Illumin8...................................169

A Note from Rob...................................174

About the Author.......................................175

FOREWORD

By Bob Hostetler

ON A RECENT TRIP, I DROVE past a sizable brick church on the main street of a small town. Two flights of stone steps rose from the curb to the four large doors of the church's main entrance. On either side of the steps, a metal sign the size of a "reserved parking" sign announced: "**NO SKATEBOARDING ON CHURCH PROPERTY.**"

I can easily imagine the chain of events that led to the sign. The concrete steps and the metal railings in front of the church would have been irresistible to young skateboard enthusiasts. Their antics may have chipped the masonry and scratched the paint on the railings. They may have sometimes blocked the steps and doors. They may not have cleaned up after themselves—bottles, wrappers, cigarette butts. Perhaps worse.

I imagine something had to be done. So signs were ordered. And bolted to the front steps of the church.

As far as I could tell, the signs did the job. There were no skateboarders in sight. The church's steps were clear. Empty. Uncluttered with young people, and no signs of them having been there.

I imagine that the members of that church are relieved that their front entrance is clear of annoying skateboarders. I am also fairly confident that those church members are concerned that today's young people seem thoroughly uninterested in God, Jesus, Christianity, and church. They may even pay someone—or a succession of someones—to attract and minister to "youth." And they probably wonder why their church is getting older and smaller, year by year, while they have remained faithful to the Gospel that was "once for all delivered to the saints."

I believe that church and its leaders need this book. I believe the vast majority of churches and church leaders need this book. I believe Rob Cook's vision, passion, and wisdom are not only exactly what youth pastors and youth ministries need, but also what the church needs. Its application reaches beyond youth ministry, to the heart, to principles, values, and approaches that the church must—absolutely must—discover or rediscover in the twenty-first century. For the sake of their survival. For the sake of the Gospel. For the sake of those who haven't yet heard, don't yet know, and are waiting to meet the Man of Galilee who can touch and change and use their lives.

Bob Hostetler

Author of *The Bard and the Bible* and (with Josh McDowell) *Don't Check Your Brains at the Door*

Youthanize

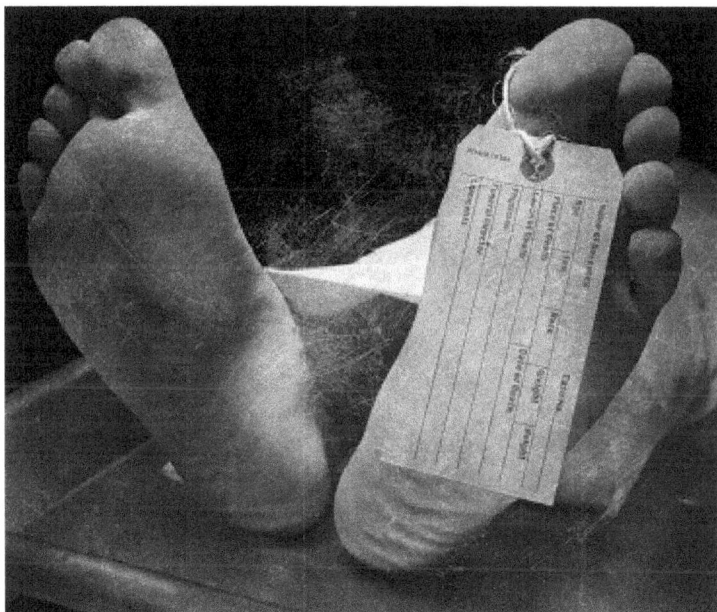

PROLOGUE

THE DEFINITION OF INSANITY, at least the street version, is doing the same thing over and over again and expecting a different result.

Could the church really be insane?

Teens outside the church are not interested in the Christian material geared towards churched kids. Ice Breakers, movie skits, games, dramas, etc.; no matter how many books we read and seminars we attend, there is a struggle to connect with unchurched teens. On top of that, the teens in our churches are walking away from God.

Why?

That's the question that punched me in the face at 11:37 p.m. as I lay in bed, fighting insomnia and questioning my mental stability.

Depending on what study you read, between 68 percent and 98 percent of all churched young people leave the church when they graduate, never to return. We've known these dire statistics for decades, yet we have not changed how we reach out to our teens in thirty years.

1

Why are we okay with a two percent retention rate? Imagine a major league baseball player only hitting the ball two times out of every hundred times at bat. What if Shaq only made two baskets out of every 100 attempts? Shaq who?

WHY ARE WE OKAY WITH A 2% RETENTION RATE?

Should we not be incredulous over these numbers? How did we get so good at turning kids off from God? Is there an *Alienating Youth 101* class or *Quitting Church for Teens* class taught at seminary?

We are failing at reaching this generation. If we don't act now, I believe the very future of Christianity is at stake, and anyone with a similar vision has to agree.

We must prevent Satan from gaining any more ground. We must fight the good fight. "*From the days of John the Baptist until now, the kingdom of heaven has been subjected to violence, and violent people have been raiding it.*" (Matthew 11:12)

Following Christ is exciting and it's time we passed that abundant adventure on. Our teens' lives are at stake. If you are sick of losing young people, passionate about changing the way things are done, and ready to impact lives for eternity, read on. It's time to **YOUTHANIZE** the old ways of reaching out to teens. The future of God's kingdom depends on it.

1

The Diagnosis

I BELIEVE GOD SENT THOSE three teenagers I found huddled on my porch in the dark to solidify my calling and the need for the ministry of *252 Underground*. When I think back to that night, which I often do in times of self-doubt and struggles, it gives me the strength to forge ahead. God stepped in and completely wrecked my self-absorbed life. It was a pivotal moment. It reset my purpose and existence.

I was sitting in my living room talking with my wife and a pastor friend who was interested in helping us with the ministry. At 9:30 p.m. the doorbell rang and I opened the door to find T.R. and B. standing there with another teen I will call S.B. I remembered promising my wife if she allowed me to have the youth ministry in our home, I would only have teens over on Friday night. We needed to set these boundaries to preserve a healthy family life. I stepped out on the porch pulling the door shut. I whispered, "What are you guys doing here? It's Saturday night, we're not open." T.R. asked me a question I will never forget. "Will you pray for my friend S.B?" He pointed to the other boy I hadn't met yet. "His father killed himself two hours ago and he found the body."

There I stood, in the dark with three boys, three weeks into a new ministry, faced with a tragic situation. In that moment I wondered where they would have gone if I had not started this ministry. Where would they have gone if I had not obeyed God? I invited them in and prayed silently to God for wisdom and direction. I was just an ordinary guy who painted houses for a living. I never went to Bible College, or any college for that matter, unless two weeks at Tampa Community College counts. I was not a Bible scholar. I didn't even know all the books in the Bible.

But none of that mattered because God knew all that and He was in control. The six of us gathered in our little living room. As I sought God's direction, I felt Him directing me to talk to B. and not S.B. (the boy who had just lost his father). It didn't make sense, but it didn't have to. If God orchestrated all this, I was going to keep obeying Him. I spoke to B. for two hours. T.R. and S.B listened intently. My wife and pastor friend sat quietly, just as amazed as I was at what God was doing.

At 11:30 p.m., after laying out the simple truths of the gospel, I asked B. if there was any reason he would not want to turn from his life of sin and commit his life to Christ. B. said there was no reason he could think of not to accept Jesus. I told him we were going to pray, and he informed me he had never prayed before. I told him I would pray and he could repeat the words after me.

I shared with him that just saying a prayer would not change him. He had to mean it in his heart. I asked him if he understood this and would he like to pray with me? He said yes, but before we could start two hands raised. "Excuse me sir. Could we say that prayer too?" That night, in a dimly lit living room on Richardson Avenue three boys gave their hearts to Jesus.

> JUST SAYING A PRAYER WOULD NOT CHANGE HIM. HE HAD TO MEAN IT IN HIS HEART.

S.B. asked me to go with him to his father's funeral, and I did. He sat with me, and I knew right then and there I would do everything I could for the young people I came across until God called me home.

2 5 2   U n d e r g r o u n d

Imagine a place you could go to where you'd be loved and accepted, right where you were, regardless of your past. What if you met people at this place who genuinely cared about you? What if you could tell them anything without fear of rejection? What if you experienced unconditional love? What if these strange people fed you when you were hungry, bought you new sneakers when duct tape no longer held yours together, and laughed and cried with you? What if you found something that seemed more like family than your own?

There is a group of young people in a small town in Pennsylvania that got to experience this through *252 Underground*.

Our house filled every Friday night with teens looking for acceptance and love. I played video games with them and listened to their stories. My wife made and served more French fries than McDonald's. We never looked back.

252 Underground was birthed in 2004. During that time, I've had the privilege to work with some of the most dedicated, selfless people. I've come to know and love hundreds of teenagers as my own children. Some I've seen grow into adulthood, graduate, get jobs or go to college. I'm proud of them. Of course, some have not changed and they continue to get into trouble, but I know seeds were planted and the word of the Lord does not return void.

I hope to inspire you with the things God has accomplished through me in the ministry of *252 Underground*. God has revealed to me effective ways to reach young people, not only in my community, but yours as well. You will hear some of the story of *252 Underground*, but it's so much more than that. This book is a training manual, to be read, studied, highlighted and, most importantly, put into practice. This book is also a journey, one I trust you will find full of adventure. My hope and prayer is that it inspires you, whether you're a seasoned youth worker or one who feels called of God to embark on the adventure of reaching teens for Christ.

I do not have all the answers, but I can tell you from my experience what works and what definitely does not. Some things might seem obvious to you, but I assure you, just because something seems obvious does not necessarily mean someone is doing it.

Just the mention of the words "youth ministry" or "youth group" can send the toughest adults running. My past experiences conjure up images of damp church basements, dimly lit corridors, and felt boards with cut-out Bible characters. There have been many advances in the area of youth ministry resources, yet unfortunately there are still many churches resisting change. These churches have become stagnant, irrelevant breeding grounds of contempt among young people. This is a harsh but true statement. Having said that, I want to make it clear that I love the established church, and I love the body of Christ. But I do not always love their methods. This "if it ain't broke don't fix it" mindset has caused an epidemic of godless teenagers who are being dragged away into captivity by the enemy.

At first I thought, writing this book would be an easy task since I've been involved in youth ministry in some form or another for a third of my life. I started *252 Underground* from scratch, and I assumed that since I had lived it, it would be a no-brainer. But how does one transcribe the work of the Holy Spirit and his life-changing power? How do you write about the sacrificial love that goes into every part of ministry and not just write a step-by-step ho- to guide: if you do a, b & c then 1, 2 & 3 will happen?

Doubt crept in daily. Who was I to think I had anything of value to impart to others about how to reach teens for Christ?

As I put things in perspective, I understood that my feelings of doubt and low self-worth were coming from Satan. He did not want this book to be written because he knows what is possible if this generation will call on Jesus, turn from their sins, and devote themselves to changing the world for Christ.

The Holy Spirit gave me a verse and I embraced it:

> *Brothers and sisters, think of what you were when you were called. Not many of you were wise by human standards; not many were influential; not many were of noble birth. But God chose the foolish things of the world to shame the wise; God chose the weak things of the world to shame the strong. God chose the lowly things of this world and the despised things—and the things that are not—to nullify the things that are, so that no one may boast before him.*
>
> *—1 Corinthians 1:26-29*

God uses the foolish things of this world. I was greatly encouraged because that described me. He put that in there just for me. This is not an attempt at humility. This is a fact, and I just want to put that on the table for those of you who feel called by God to do something, but feel unworthy and unqualified. We are all unworthy, but God uses us because He is merciful, full of grace, and He loves us.

There are many more-intelligent people capable of completing the vision that God has placed in your heart. Yet He sees and desires to use you. He created you expressly for that purpose, and He will empower you. Look at the people He chose to use in the Bible. They may be great men and women of history now, but that was certainly not the case when God first came calling. Moses was a stuttering murderer. David was a teenage shepherd boy. Nehemiah was the cupbearer to the King. Peter was an uneducated fisherman.

> THERE ARE MANY MORE-INTELLIGENT PEOPLE CAPABLE OF COMPLETING THE VISION THAT GOD HAS PLACED IN YOUR HEART. YET HE SEES AND DESIRES TO USE YOU.

I think you get the picture.

If a great man accomplishes something for God, the great man gets all the glory. But if a foolish man allows God to accomplish something great through him, God gets all the glory.

The priests and the captain of the temple guard and the Sadducees came up to Peter and John while they were speaking to the people. They were greatly disturbed because the apostles were teaching the people, proclaiming in Jesus the resurrection of the dead. They seized Peter and John and, because it was evening, they put them in jail until the next day. But many who heard the message believed; so the number of men who believed grew to about five thousand.

The next day the rulers, the elders and the teachers of the law met in Jerusalem. Annas the high priest was there, and so were Caiaphas, John, Alexander and others of the high priest's family. They had Peter and John brought before them and began to question them: "By what power or what name did you do this?"

Then Peter, filled with the Holy Spirit, said to them: "Rulers and elders of the people! If we are being called to account today for an act of kindness shown to a man who was lame and are being asked how he was healed, then know this, you and all the people of Israel: It is by the name of Jesus Christ of Nazareth, whom you crucified but whom God raised from the dead, that this man stands before you healed. Jesus is

> *'the stone you builders rejected,*
> *which has become the cornerstone.'*

Salvation is found in no one else, for there is no other name under heaven given to mankind by which we must be saved."

When they saw the courage of Peter and John and realized that they were unschooled, ordinary men, they were astonished and they took note that these men had been with Jesus. But since they could see the man who had been healed standing there with them, there was nothing they could say. So they ordered them to withdraw from the Sanhedrin and then conferred together. "What are we going to do with these men?" they asked. "Everyone living in Jerusalem knows they have performed a notable sign, and we cannot deny it. But to stop this thing from spreading any further among the people, we must warn them to speak no longer to anyone in this name."

Then they called them in again and commanded them not to speak or teach at all in the name of Jesus. But Peter and John replied, "Which is right in God's eyes: to listen to you, or to him? You be the judges! As for us, we cannot help speaking about what we have seen and heard."

After further threats they let them go. They could not decide how to punish them, because all the people were praising God for what had happened.

—*Acts 4:1-21*

Peter and John are teaching and proclaiming in the name of Jesus. The Sanhedrin, wise men by the world's standards, were upset with Peter and John and brought them in to be interrogated. They asked, "By what power or in what name do you preach these things?" Peter was a lowly fisherman but filled with the Holy Spirit, and he proceeded to "school" the religious leaders and gave Jesus all the glory. Verse 13 says, "When they saw the courage of Peter and John and realized that they were unschooled, ordinary men, they were astonished and they took note that these men had been with Jesus."

I'd rather God get the glory, as I am sure you would too.

When you strip everything else away, that is what God is really looking for. He is looking for anyone willing to surrender their life completely to His will and commit unwaveringly to carrying out the vision He has placed in their heart—the purpose for which they were created.

This is the story of God using the foolish and of how *252 Underground* Youth Ministry came to be. It is a story of God's miraculous provision and mercy.

2

What's in Your Tackle Box?

I'M A PAINTER BY TRADE, and I always keep my eye open for innovative products that will help me do a better job more quickly and efficiently. I figure if I can get the job done better and faster, then the customer will be happy and I will make more money. It's a win/win situation.

I often wonder why we as a church don't have the same philosophy regarding youth ministry. When youth pastors want to try new techniques that are relevant to today's youth they are often bombarded with phrases like, "We've always done it like this, we've never done it like that," or "When I was a kid we didn't need all that."

What if I looked at my painting business with the same mindset? I use brushes and rollers, and on some occasions I even use a sprayer. Talk about painting quickly. But what if some old-timer saw me using a roller and said, "Back in my day, all we had were paint brushes. We didn't need any fancy rollers or sprayers." My brush does a great job cutting in or painting trim. Does that mean I should not use a roller? If I were to brush out all the walls and ceiling in a room, it would take forever... and it would not look as nice. A brush has a specific purpose but doesn't come close to what a roller can do. It's a great invention.

It's the same with youth ministry. The old ways of doing things worked at a specific time and served a specific purpose, but times have changed and what worked in 1950 does not work today.

Just like what the roller did for painting, new advancements in technology allow us to reach more teens with greater efficiency.

NEW ADVANCEMENTS IN TECHNOLOGY ALLOW US TO REACH MORE TEENS WITH GREATER EFFICIENCY.

Facebook allows me the opportunity to reach hundreds of kids with one click of a mouse. Offering the latest video game draws a massive crowd and provides a captive audience to share the gospel message with.

Jesus called us to be fishers of men for a reason. He could have used any number of metaphors, but he chose fishing. We can learn a lot from observing professional fishermen. Adaptability for starters. After fishing for a while without any bites, a professional fisherman will change the bait. He will continue to search until he finds something the fish will nibble on.

Unfortunately, most churches don't follow this simple yet proven method. We use techniques, bait if you will, that worked twenty, thirty, or even forty years ago. Then we sit around and wonder why we are not making an impact on our youth. Why aren't the "fish" nibbling? We throw up our hands and come to the conclusion the youth of today are just not interested in God. Shame on us. I've heard it said that the greatest enemy of future success is often the successes of the past.

Please don't misunderstand me. The gospel never changes. Jesus is the same yesterday, today, and forever. The bait is the only thing that changes, and we need to understand this to remain effective in the battle for souls.

I drove this point home recently when speaking at a church with a relatively small youth group. I asked this question, "Do you believe that Jesus is the same yesterday, today and forever?" Every head nodded in agreement as I fully expected. I then explained how two thousand years ago people of all ages (teens too), followed Jesus for days at a time; forsaking food, shelter, comfort, and their MP3 players. (Well, maybe just because they hadn't been invented yet.) The people hung on His every word. I asked them if this were true. Every head bobbed; they agreed wholeheartedly with this truth. I then dropped a reality bomb and asked: "If Jesus is the same yesterday, today and forever and people in fact followed Him for days at a time forsaking food, shelter and comfort, hanging on His every word ... then how come when we jump forward two thousand years, we can't keep the interest of teenagers for an hour?" One tiny hour, sixty little minutes in climate-controlled comfort, with donuts to munch on and hot coffee to wash them down. We even provide comfortable seating in place of a rocky hillside. And yet we can't get them to come hear the same message Jesus preached.

If Jesus has not changed, then what's wrong with this picture?

Here's the answer, and make sure you catch this: It's the way the church presents Jesus. The Word of God—the gospel—is the hook, but they are not nibbling on the hook of the gospel because they don't like the bait. It does not taste good in their mouth. For whatever reason, maybe the smell or texture, something is wrong.

I'll say it again; the word of God is the hook, but so often we use the wrong bait. Professional fishermen use the right bait for the type of fish they plan to catch. They would never use worms to go shark fishing. Never.

Sadly, when we go fishing for souls, most times in our minds, we don't plan on catching anything. When I was speaking at another church on this subject, I asked them what they would need to take on a fishing trip. I got the obvious answers you'd expect: fishing rod, boat, hooks, and bait. But no one, not one person out of five-hundred, said a bucket. When I mentioned this fact, they looked at me with blank stares. What's the bucket for? The fish you plan on catching. You need a big bucket to hold all the fish you plan to catch. Most people don't take a bucket because they don't plan on catching anything.

When a professional fisherman goes fishing, he plans on catching fish. He comes prepared. He has the vest with all the lures and different kinds of bait. He brings different kinds of rods with different size hooks. He's got the big net and hip waders. In anticipation of all the fish he plans on catching, he brings a big cooler full of ice to pack the fish in for the trip home.

As a church, too often we are like the guy who comes to the same lake with the cheapest rod and a big ball of tangled string. We use rubber worms with rusted dull hooks, fish for a little while, then quit in frustration. We say the fish aren't biting. The lake needs to be stocked. We make excuses for our failure, while the pro in the same "un-stocked" lake is reeling in one after another.

This is often the mindset we as a church have when we fish for the souls of teenagers. Out of duty we cast a line with outdated, unattractive bait.

Let's look at a typical church organized outreach—the famous, or should I say infamous, *GYM LOCK IN*. The church youth band plays worship songs that praise Jesus and proclaims our undying devotion and surrender to Him. This is followed by some games, most of which are corny. Up next is a Bible message that notifies the teens of their need of a Savior since they are lost and on their way to hell. Queue the worship music for dramatic effect as the young people decide whether they want to join the club or burn for eternity.

Everyone has great intentions. Everyone truly wants to reach teenagers for Jesus. But the reality is, the lock-ins are attended by churched teens that have been raised in the church and already know the pitch. They love Jesus or at least act as if they do. They know all the words to the songs and they know that we sing the chorus twenty-seven times and don't find it at all weird. They get to stay up all night and hang out with their other church friends who know they are a Christian, so no need to be embarrassed. They can be themselves.

Now picture yourself as an unchurched teen coming to this same "outreach."

Would you feel comfortable singing to this Jesus whom you don't know? Would you want to tell Him how you'll live only for Him, how you'll surrender all? Would you be at ease telling Him how you love, adore, and worship Him and how you long to know Him more intimately?

Would you want to be told you're lost and that you need to accept this Jesus who you don't know anything about? We tell them it's no accident that they're here. This could be their last chance. If they die without saying this prayer, this loving Jesus who they wanted you to sing to, is going to throw you into hell and burn you for eternity. Praise the Lord. Let's have snacks.

Is that how you came to Christ? Is that how we build meaningful lasting relationships with Christ-devoted followers who can evangelize their peers? Every week, somewhere in America these type of "outreaches" go on in churches, and while they may be well meaning they are ineffective. More often than not our intentions to bring teens to Christ through these methods produce the opposite effect.

WOULD YOU WANT TO BE TOLD YOU'RE LOST AND THAT YOU NEED TO ACCEPT THIS JESUS WHO YOU DON'T KNOW ANYTHING ABOUT?

If you are reading these words and have been involved in this sort of "outreach," don't beat yourself up. God knows your heart. I'm just glad that you have the desire to reach young people. It is my desire that this book be used in conjunction with the vision God has placed in your heart. I hope that we can partner together in these pages to refine what you are currently doing and make it more meaningful and effective. It is my hope and prayer this book becomes an invaluable tool in creating a positive and effective outreach in your community and you, the reader, are able to disciple and mentor many teens.

Discussion Points

- Jesus loved people, cared about them, met their needs, and taught them in practical, interesting ways. We tell people to say a prayer or burn in hell.

- What can you do this week to be more in line with the Jesus model of relational evangelism?

- What relevant bait can you add to your tackle box to be more effective in catching "fish"?

3

Get   in   the   Water

PREVIOUSLY, I SHARED HOW A fisherman stood on the river's edge and cast his hook into the water. Since the fish didn't come to him, he got frustrated and gave up, blaming his failure to catch anything on the fish not biting, the lake needing to be stocked, and a thousand other reasons why he wasn't successful.

The professional fisherman, on the other hand, comes prepared, puts on his hip waders and goes out to where the fish are. He is passionate about fishing. He chooses his bait carefully and patiently waits, knowing it takes time. The fish will need to eat sooner or later. He doesn't give up easily. He doesn't make excuses. His perseverance pays off. He walks away with a full bucket from the same lake that "failed" the average fisherman.

Most church youth outreach organizations fish with a bullhorn. They stand in the boat and scream at the fish to get into the boat. It doesn't work on the fish, and it doesn't work on teens.

To have an effective outreach, you need to do some research. Don't ask your church kids what they would like. Find out what's hot with unchurched kids. This is your target market. When you find out what they are into, that will be your bait. It's not rocket science. Teens love music, video games, Doritos®, and Mountain Dew®.

> TO HAVE AN EFFECTIVE OUTREACH, YOU NEED TO DO SOME RESEARCH. FIND OUT WHAT'S HOT WITH UNCHURCHED KIDS.

Many well-meaning church folks have criticized our methods at *252 Underground.* They ask me why we use video games to reach kids. They question why we give away soda when water is healthier for them. They say we should feed them fruit instead of candy bars. The music we play is too fast and they suggest we teach them church hymns instead.

Let me tell you why we do what we do. Picture this: After weeks of hype and advertising and countless hours preparing an outreach event to unchurched kids, the big day finally arrives. We are pumped and ready. Every detail has been covered by an army of dedicated volunteers. Counselors stand by for all the teens that are going to say "the prayer" tonight. We have our follow-up committee in place. Our prayer partners are meeting in the church basement calling on the Holy Spirit to move teens' hearts. Nothing has been left to chance.

The teens show up and upon entering they hear the *Old Rugged Cross* pumping through the speakers. They shoot straight to the food table to discover bottles of water and a nice bowl of apples and oranges. How many minutes do you think it would take for them to clear out, text all their friends, and warn them to avoid your "outreach" like the plague? Some of you know what I'm talking about; others should be glad you don't.

You blew it. Your team is discouraged. You have to give a report to the senior pastor—your boss—at the weekly meeting and explain why, after spending all the time and resources, you have nothing to show for it. Worse than that, you've earned a bad reputation with the teens in your community, and will be hard pressed to get them to return to your next "outreach."

"Do your research. Know your market," as they say in business, and with good reason. If you were reaching out to the Jews in your community you would not serve pork for dinner.

Here is an example of a sure-fire outreach success:

You see a group of teens skating near your church on a regular basis. You decide to connect with them, but how? Go to Zumiez, a skateboard store, or any store like it. Find DVDs of the latest skateboarders doing their thing. Ask the clerk which one is the best and buy it. I'm sure you have a few dollars in your youth budget. If not, check the couch cushions. Find a couple of people who are good at applying grip tape to skateboards. If you don't know what that is, find out.

Go out to Sam's Club or Costco. Buy cases of Mountain Dew®and boxes of those mini bags of Doritos® and Snickers® bars. Pick a night to host the event. Run some cool looking postcards off on your church copier and go pass them out to the skaters. They will tell all their friends, trust me. Set up your gym or sanctuary to show the DVD. Serve the drinks and food. After the movie, apply the grip tape to the skateboards, and you're in business. You have made friends for life.

Here's the hard part: resist the urge to share the gospel that night. What you are doing is relational evangelism. Jesus was the Master of this method. If you try to preach to them that night, they will see it as a bait and switch setup. Teens are smart, and they will feel you did all this just to shove the gospel down their throat. They don't know you, and you haven't earned the right to be heard yet ... but it's a start. You thank them for coming and tell them you are looking forward to getting to know them. This will blow them away because they might have expected you to preach at them. You will earn their respect.

That first night make sure you have another event planned with postcards to hand out. For your next outreach bring in a skater willing to give his/her testimony, nothing over the top. Feed them again and let them know you are there if they need you and that you care.

This is not a hit and run method. This is about building lasting relationships. This isn't about numbers and how many kids "said a prayer" and "raised their hand." You want kids that, when they accept Christ, mean it, understand it, and make a decision for the long haul.

When a missionary goes to another country with a different culture, they move into the communities and live among the people. They don't show up and start preaching the gospel. They know that doesn't work. They get jobs and learn the culture, make friends, and gain the trust and respect of the people; usually a two or three-year endeavor.

When the time comes to share their faith, it feels natural and is accepted more readily. The people trust the missionaries, and whole communities are affected and changed.

Why do we feel we can bypass this proven method when reaching out to teenagers? Why do we use methods that are more like shotgun fishing? All that does is make a lot of noise, scare the fish away, and kill a few.

Get in the water.

D i s c u s s i o n   P o i n t s

- What are some of the areas in your town that young people gravitate to?

- What is it about these places that attract them?

- If you were to perform an honest assessment of your previous youth outreach efforts, would you find they were geared towards churched teens more than unchurched teens?

- Now if you did your research for question one and you know where young people tend to gather, do this: Take some pizzas and sodas to this location and just drop them off (when the kids are there, of course). Tape your card to the top of the pizza boxes.

- Do this more than once.

4

Be a Rope Holder

AS WE STUDY THE GOSPEL we read that Jesus did not approve of all the people did, but He accepted them where they were and loved them too much to leave them there. That's the way we approach youth ministry at *252 Underground.* We do not approve of teens smoking or drinking. We don't approve of their drug use. We don't approve of the fact that they are sexually active. But we love them.

It's been said, Jesus called us to be fishers of men not cleaners of fish, but that's what the church is attempting today. We want the fish cleaned, gutted, and the scales removed. We will never reach anyone that way. We are to catch them; it's the Holy Spirit's job to clean them up. Our job is to be a GPS and simply point the way to Christ.

Let's look at two examples of this method in Scripture. Look at this passage:

> *Now he had to go through Samaria. So he came to a town in Samaria called Sychar, near the plot of ground Jacob had given to his son Joseph. Jacob's well was there, and Jesus, tired as he was from the journey, sat down by the well. It was about noon.*
>
> *When a Samaritan woman came to draw water, Jesus said to her, "Will you give me a drink?" (His disciples had gone into the town to buy food.)*
>
> *The Samaritan woman said to him, "You are a Jew and I am a Samaritan woman. How can you ask me for a drink?" (For Jews do not associate with Samaritans.)*
>
> *Jesus answered her, "If you knew the gift of God and who it is that asks you for a drink, you would have asked him and he would have given you living water."*
>
> *"Sir," the woman said, "you have nothing to draw with and the well is deep. Where can you get this living water? Are you greater than our father Jacob, who gave us the well and drank from it himself, as did also his sons and his livestock?"*
>
> *Jesus answered, "Everyone who drinks this water will be thirsty again, but whoever drinks the water I give them will*

never thirst. Indeed, the water I give them will become in them a spring of water welling up to eternal life."

The woman said to him, "Sir, give me this water so that I won't get thirsty and have to keep coming here to draw water."

He told her, "Go, call your husband and come back."

"I have no husband," she replied.

Jesus said to her, "You are right when you say you have no husband. The fact is, you have had five husbands, and the man you now have is not your husband. What you have just said is quite true."

"Sir," the woman said, "I can see that you are a prophet. Our ancestors worshiped on this mountain, but you Jews claim that the place where we must worship is in Jerusalem."

"Woman," Jesus replied, "believe me, a time is coming when you will worship the Father neither on this mountain nor in Jerusalem. You Samaritans worship what you do not know; we worship what we do know, for salvation is from the Jews. Yet a time is coming and has now come when the true worshipers will worship the Father in the Spirit and in truth, for they are the kind of worshipers the Father seeks. God is spirit, and his worshipers must worship in the Spirit and in truth."

The woman said, "I know that Messiah" (called Christ) "is coming. When he comes, he will explain everything to us."

Then Jesus declared, "I, the one speaking to you—I am he."

Just then his disciples returned and were surprised to find him talking with a woman. But no one asked, "What do you want?" or "Why are you talking with her?"

Then, leaving her water jar, the woman went back to the town and said to the people, "Come, see a man who told me everything I ever did. Could this be the Messiah?" They came out of the town and made their way toward him.

Meanwhile his disciples urged him, "Rabbi, eat something."

But he said to them, "I have food to eat that you know nothing about."

Then his disciples said to each other, "Could someone have brought him food?"

"My food," said Jesus, "is to do the will of him who sent me and to finish his work. Don't you have a saying, 'It's still four months until harvest'? I tell you, open your eyes and look at the fields! They are ripe for harvest. Even now the one who reaps draws a wage and harvests a crop for eternal life, so that the sower and the reaper may be glad together. Thus the saying 'One sows and another reaps' is true. I sent

you to reap what you have not worked for. Others have done the hard work, and you have reaped the benefits of their labor."

Many of the Samaritans from that town believed in him because of the woman's testimony, "He told me everything I ever did." So when the Samaritans came to him, they urged him to stay with them, and he stayed two days. And because of his words many more became believers.

They said to the woman, "We no longer believe just because of what you said; now we have heard for ourselves, and we know that this man really is the Savior of the world."

—John 4:4-42

Jesus had to go through Samaria. Jews never traveled through Samaria. They despised Samaritans, and in an effort to avoid them they would travel eastward the long way around. But it says Jesus had to go to Samaria. That tells me Jesus deliberately sought out this woman. It's why the fisherman puts waders on and gets into the water; he goes where the fish are.

Jesus set the example for His disciples. They needed to learn how to witness not only in Jerusalem and Judea, but in Samaria as well. He forced them outside their comfort zone.

L e s s o n   1 :
C o m f o r t   Z o n e

We need to get out of our comfort zone and go to the places where the people who need Christ live, places we tend to avoid, and talk to people we would normally steer clear of. Samaritans and Jews were enemies, but Jesus commands us to love our enemies. What better way to show love than to introduce someone to Christ?

Jesus knew the stigma between Jews and Samaritans, and yet He asked the woman for a drink. Jews refused to share utensils with Samaritans for fear of ritual contamination. That was what legalism looked like in biblical times.

L e s s o n   2 :
I n t e r a c t

We need to actually interact with people who are questionable (in our minds). Today it may be fear of shaking a dirty homeless man's hand or not wanting to associate with a group of foul-mouthed teens.

This Samaritan woman was considered an outcast and was ashamed. She came to the well in the afternoon heat to avoid the harsh comments and judgmental stares of others. She had been married five times and was now living with a man she was not married to. The Jews did not approve of her sin. This is why many avoid the church today.

Jesus went out of His way to reach her, and when He found her He didn't tear her down or berate her. He could have, and He would have been within His rights, but he dangled a little bait in front of her. He piqued her curiosity.

L e s s o n   3 :   B a i t

Figure out what bait will work. It's like fishing for shark. You attract them by throwing chum in the water. Sharks can smell blood in the water from miles away. Their need for food brings them close, and while they are feeding, a baited hook can be slipped in among the chum. The sharks don't feel threatened and eventually find the hook.

Incidentally but not accidentally, this is the very reason we use free video games and snacks as bait. Word spreads like wildfire through social media and texts. I reiterate this point because it's key to reaching young people and it is so important that you get this.

Jesus employed the same technique with the woman at the well. He recognized her need, and met her there. As she drew water, he spoke to her of Living water. He throws out his bait, and she nibbles. Where can she get this living water? She needs and wants it. Jesus reveals Himself to her and she believes.

Now remember, she is the town adulterer. She is not a Bible scholar. She is not a teacher or religious leader. Take note of the verses when she goes back to the town and convinces the people to also meet Jesus. She was the GPS pointing the way to Jesus. The key is this verse: "Many of the Samaritans believed in Him because of the woman's testimony, 'He told me everything I ever did.'" That statement piqued their curiosity—it was bait. Her personal testimony was simple yet powerful. The men of the city went out to meet Jesus and urged him to stay with them. The passage ends by saying "And because of His (Jesus') words, many more became believers."

The woman simply pointed to Jesus, and Jesus did what He does best. The woman didn't try to convert anyone. She didn't get into theological disputes over doctrine or try to change anyone. She simply introduced them to Jesus the Master. Let Jesus do His job. You do yours. It's easy—just point.

What's Your Reason?

The Bible exhorts us to "*be ready to give the reason for the hope that is in you, in season and out.*" (1 Peter 3:15) Whether you're weary, busy, or tired. Jesus had traveled almost forty miles through the desert heat. He was exhausted, hungry, and thirsty, yet He witnessed to this woman, an outcast, and through her testimony many came to the saving knowledge of Jesus Christ.

Remember not to prejudge or attempt to prequalify anyone. If you saw the town whore at the local watering hole, would you have shared the gospel with her? Would you have thought there was a chance she would be interested? That she desperately needed what you have to offer? Or would you have written her off, decided she wouldn't be interested? Please get this critical fact; we are not called to judge any man, woman, or teen. We are simply called to be witnesses.

The second example I want to share with you is found in this passage:

> *A few days later, when Jesus again entered Capernaum, the people heard that he had come home. They gathered in such large numbers that there was no room left, not even outside the door, and he preached the word to them. Some men came, bringing to him a paralyzed man, carried by four of them. Since they could not get him to Jesus because of the crowd, they made an opening in the roof above Jesus by digging through it and then lowered the mat the man was lying on. When Jesus saw their faith, he said to the paralyzed man, "Son, your sins are forgiven."*

Now some teachers of the law were sitting there, thinking to themselves, "Why does this fellow talk like that? He's blaspheming! Who can forgive sins but God alone?"

Immediately Jesus knew in his spirit that this was what they were thinking in their hearts, and he said to them, "Why are you thinking these things? Which is easier: to say to this paralyzed man, 'Your sins are forgiven,' or to say, 'Get up, take your mat and walk'? But I want you to know that the Son of Man has authority on earth to forgive sins." So he said to the man, "I tell you, get up, take your mat and go home."

—*Mark 2:1-11*

Jesus was in Capernaum. The crowds heard He was there and they found where He was staying. Hundreds of people in need of healing converged on the house, and there was no room left, not even outside the door. A group of four men had heard Jesus the healer was in town so they got their friend, a paralytic, and made their way to see Jesus. When they arrived at the house, they saw no way to get their friend close to Jesus, but they believed that an encounter with Jesus would forever change the quality of their friend's life. They were determined to facilitate that connection by any means necessary so their friend would be healed. All they had to do was get him close to Jesus, and Jesus would do the rest.

When all hope seemed lost, the task daunting, the massive crowd an overwhelming obstacle; they refused to quit. They climbed up on the roof and tore a hole in it, fastened ropes to the corners of their friend's mat, and lowered him through the hole and close to Jesus. When Jesus saw the efforts of these four men and their faith, he was moved to compassion and healed the paralytic.

The men were not doctors, but they knew the Great Physician. All they had to do was get their friend close to Jesus. Same for us. That's what we do at *252 Underground.* We hold the rope so teens can get close to Jesus.

W h a t   W e   D o   M a t t e r s

I found an awesome rope holder in Jim Voight.

I started attending my mother's church when Jim was the youth pastor. When I met Jim, the first thing that popped into my mind was, *if he's the pastor why does he have long hair?* The Christian schools I had attended told me that to be a Christian, you had to have short hair. Hadn't anyone told Jim?

Jim was the coolest guy I ever met. He was funny and had a huge heart for God. He had this awesome youth ministry that was growing and the kids loved him—but more importantly they loved God. Jim was doing something that made these kids love God, so I figured God would overlook the fact that Jim had long hair.

I found myself drawn to Jim and wanted to hang out with him. He made me want to serve God with all my heart. I started to think Jesus was probably like that. He loved people and cared for them, and people wanted to be around him.

Jim was the first "Jesus" I ever saw. When I was growing up in Lansdale, I was a troubled youth (massive understatement). I can honestly say no one from a church ever approached me. I was surrounded by churches and no one ever shared Jesus with me. My dad walked out on us when I was seven years old. I went through years filled with anger, frustration, and depression. I often wonder how different my life could have been if someone like Jim had taken an interest in me when I was younger. Even now, as an adult, I wanted to be just like Jim and that meant being just like Jesus.

I OFTEN THINK NOW HOW DIFFERENT MY LIFE COULD HAVE BEEN IF SOMEONE LIKE JIM HAD TAKEN AN INTEREST IN ME.

Jim wasn't your normal pastor. At least what I, an unchurched thirty-year-old, thought a pastor should look like. He was funny, crazy, and came up with the coolest games teenagers loved. He made Bible stories come alive. I started to believe these ancient people actually lived and did the things the Bible said they did.

Jim cared about every kid that came through the door. It didn't matter what you looked like, what music you listened to, how long your hair was, or even what color it was for that matter.

As I started to work with Jim in the youth ministry, my faith continued to grow stronger. Without even realizing it a seed had been planted in me.

The knowledge in my head became the passion in my heart. The walls I built to protect myself started to crack as the Holy Spirit broke through. As I saw God's purpose for my life more clearly, everything started to make sense.

I came to the realization that God allowed all these things to happen to me so I would be able to deal with the ministry he was preparing me for. Just like God allowed Joseph to suffer all those setbacks so He could use him to bring about his plan for the children of Israel.

I made a decision to surrender my life wholly to Christ, to do whatever He required of me, and to go wherever He sent me. God started speaking to me, and His desires became mine—His will my will.

As a volunteer, I started helping Jim with his Friday night youth program. I watched Jim closely and saw how he connected with the teens who came to the church.

As I grew closer to God in my faith, I began to understand that He desired reconciliation between Himself and the lost. The more I grasped this, the more I felt the need to reach the teens that were not coming through the door of the church—the teens who truly needed to hear about this God who loved them unconditionally. I could relate to them because I'd been just like them.

The challenge came when I attempted to invite them to church. After approaching them on the street, I zealously introduced myself and told them how much God loved them. Then I invited them to our youth group, but that did not go over as well as I'd hoped. The kids didn't know me from Adam and I probably came across as a nut job. For all I knew, these teens had an abusive father or alcoholic mother. Maybe they were contemplating suicide. Along comes Johnny Christian telling them Jesus loves them. But they don't even know what it feels like to be loved, let alone believe this strange dude telling them an invisible God does.

The ones who did listen and came to the church were quickly sent packing by church members who did not like the way they dressed or talked. They didn't want the teenagers to smoke on church property. I was stuck in a catch-22, or more like catch and release. I caught them and the church released them.

I CAUGHT THEM AND THE CHURCH RELEASED THEM.

The kids who needed Jesus the most, the ones who would benefit most from a church community, were turned away for not having Jesus in their life. If you're serious about reaching unchurched teens, you must be willing to put up with people who have tons of problems. Fishing is often messy and smelly.

It's like trying to establish credit. You need credit to get credit, but you can't get credit unless you have credit. See how ridiculous that sounds?

The more God burdened me with reaching these teenagers, the more disillusioned I became with the traditional church mindset. Let me say it again, I am not against the established church or the concept of church. I love the church community, the fellowship, and the discipleship that comes from being a member of the church body. But I believe the system for reaching this generation of young people is broken or at the least, severely damaged. For those of you who are worried this is a church bashing book, rest assured, it is not. My desire is to state the facts and share proven methods today's church can use to reach a generation desperately in need of Jesus.

Many of you share the same heart and want to reach these young people. Reaching this YouTube, Snapchat, Instagram, Twitter, texting, too-busy-for-some-guy-who-lived-2000-years-ago generation takes a bold vision. If we as the body of Christ don't tear down the wall the enemy has constructed between the church and today's youth, the wall will grow.

I and my friends have witnessed God do incredible things in the lives of some pretty hardcore youth. As I interviewed countless teens, and saw a lack of relevant material out there that speaks to this great need, I decided to add my voice to this vital conversation, believing it is God's desire to expand our vision.

Jesus commanded us to go into all the world and make disciples. He did not tell us to wait for them to come to us. The methods for reaching and teaching "church kids" are completely different from reaching and teaching "unchurched kids." This is why "church kids" don't invite their "unchurched" friends.

That's what I learned from Jim. He understood this. He saw what the teens were going through and related to them in a way they understood. That's why they came and brought their friends. They didn't care if Jim had short, long, or no hair. He was real, relatable, and most importantly he loved them.

Become a rope holder.

5

Equipping for Battle

IN THE PREVIOUS CHAPTER I SHARED with you that I believe God allowed certain events in my life to prepare me for the ministry He had created me for.

To explain what I mean by that, I want to take a moment to tell you about some incidents from my life that led me to a pivotal realization of God's sovereign grace and how He was orchestrating His will in my life long before I ever knew Him.

It will also help you to understand my passion and my motivation for reaching the young people in my community and the world.

My life as I live it today is a million miles and another dimension from where I came from. While that may be the case, I cling to a verse that gave it all meaning as I look back on the troubling details of my chaotic childhood.

The verse is Romans 8:28: "*And we know that in all things God works for the good of those who love him, who have been called according to His purpose.*"

What Satan intends for evil, God turns to good.

Joseph was sold into slavery, falsely accused of attempted rape, imprisoned for years, and virtually forgotten. All these events were orchestrated by God so He could have Joseph positioned at the right time and place to save the twelve tribes of Judah.

In Genesis 50:19, Joseph assures his brothers that he does not intend to harm them for the evil they did to him: *But Joseph said to them, "Don't be afraid. Am I not in the place of God? You intended to harm me, but God intended it for good to accomplish what is now being done, the saving of many lives."*

As He did for those twelve tribes, God was behind the scenes orchestrating everything in my life for such a time as this, for these kids, and for you the reader of this book.

I was born on Christmas day in 1967. My mom's first two pregnancies ended in the babies being stillborn. She became pregnant again and my brother David was born. Two years later, Merry Christmas, I arrived, and three years later my brother Rick was born.

When I was young, I was always fighting to survive. The things I am going to share with you are not intended to tear my family down but only to reveal the sovereignty of God and how He truly works for the good of those who love Him.

My father was an alcoholic and a drug user. He physically abused my mother, my brothers, and me. I won't go into all the horrific details since that's not what this book is about, but I lived in constant fear of his next attack of rage.

When I was seven years old, my father sat my mother, me, and my brothers ages nine and four, down on the sofa and told us he was leaving. He told my mother he didn't love her anymore. He told us he'd been having an ongoing affair with a man named Ralph, and he was in love with him. Although I was only seven and it was over forty years ago, I can see the scene so vividly it may as well have happened this morning.

Up until this point I had never heard of God or had ever been to a church. I didn't have any peace beyond all understanding—only anger, confusion, and fear.

> I DIDN'T HAVE ANY PEACE BEYOND ALL UNDERSTANDING; ONLY ANGER, CONFUSION AND FEAR.

Although that was a traumatic event and a turning point in my young life, it was followed by many more equally traumatic circumstances. My mother was deaf and had no income, and she became extremely depressed. She and my father had been high school sweethearts. She loved him, and to this day, still does. He was her soul mate, the one she thought she would grow old with, but her dreams were derailed in 1975.

My dad paid no child support and we could no longer afford our apartment so had to move. My family got divided among friends—whoever had space for us. I was only seven years old and separated from my mother. I was bitter. I started wetting the sofa I slept on at night.

Embarrassed, self-conscious, and ashamed, I hated my life and my dad for what he did to us. At that time, I didn't care if I lived or died. Seven-year-olds should be worrying about simpler things, like who they want to dress up as for Halloween, or what flavor ice cream is the best. I worried if there would be food to eat, if we would have a place to live, if Santa would find me at Shirley's house?

My mom finally started to receive public assistance, food stamps, and government cheese, and we got a small apartment in Lansdale, Pennsylvania.

Although we had the basics we didn't have much else. Even our Christmas presents came from the Lansdale Police Department. Unlike today where people donate a new unused toy to *Toys for Tots*, back in the 70's the toys were used toys. We didn't care, though. I can remember being so excited every year waiting for them to come. An officer, dressed up like Santa, would deliver our presents and we would scream with joy. The local food pantry, *Manna on Main Street*, (still in existence today), would bring the turkey and all the fixings. I was, and remain, so grateful to them for their love, kindness, and willingness to be so generous.

But as small boys we still wanted more. We wanted the life we saw other kids living. We wanted bicycles and Atari video games with PacMan and asteroids. Those things were out of the question—just a dream. But then we found a way to make them a reality. My brother David, an up-and-coming criminal mastermind, came up with the idea to take from the rich and give to the poor, namely us. He always had a way of persuasion (more like a gift). He'd convince Rick and I, seven and eleven respectively, of his foolproof plans, so at our tender ages we began a life of crime which continued well into our twenties.

I was arrested at eleven for breaking and entering. I was arrested for theft, and arrested for fighting. The fights were because people made fun of us for the clothes we wore. My mother and grandmother would purchase our "new" school clothes from the Goodwill store—all you could fit in a brown grocery bag for $2.00. On top of that I had poor vision, and welfare only paid for the glasses no one else wanted—dark brown horn-rimmed glasses. The kids at school were brutal. I hated life in a whole new way.

Then, as I became a teenager, God started to reveal himself to me in a way to this day I cannot fully explain. Something in me wanted to do good even though I struggled in the life I knew. I continued doing bad things but they bothered me.

My mom had become a Christian and had been taking us to Sunday school and church, but if I had to explain church I would say I had some head knowledge but God had not yet gotten a hold of my heart. It was like there was this power struggle going on inside me, and knowing what I know now it makes perfect sense. Satan was fighting for control of my soul and my life, but God had other plans.

> SATAN WAS FIGHTING FOR CONTROL OF MY SOUL AND MY LIFE, BUT GOD HAD OTHER PLANS.

I gave what I thought was my heart to Jesus (but it turned out to just be my mind) while attending a Christian school with money from an education fund set up when my Uncle Bill passed away.

I learned all about Jesus and went to church, but I felt like the preacher was always talking over me. The stories he told about the characters in the Bible were no more real to me than Tom Sawyer or Huck Finn. I continued in my sinful lifestyle, but felt safe and secure in the knowledge that I was going to heaven because I had prayed that little prayer.

I felt alone in my own household for many reasons and was eventually kicked out of the house by my older brother. At seventeen I was homeless, looking for love and acceptance. I wanted to be a part of a family—anyone's family. I had watched the *Brady Bunch* on television and I believed there was a family out there like that. Someday I would have a family just like that too.

Because of my insecurities and my need to be loved, I got involved with a girl and became the father of a baby girl when I was nineteen. We got married and had a son by the time I was twenty-one. And then my world fell apart, again. With both my wife and me coming from dysfunctional families and without a foundation built on Christ, we crumbled.

My broken life taunted me a thousand ways. Life was not worth living. I would never amount to anything or have the family I longed for. That is what I believed, courtesy of the devil, though I didn't know then that the devil was the father of lies. I didn't know about the passage in 1 Peter 5:8 that warns: *Your enemy the devil prowls around like a roaring lion looking for someone to devour.* I had also missed the part in verse 10 that tells us that *The God of all grace, who called you to his eternal glory in Christ, after you had suffered a little while, will himself restore you and make you strong, firm and steadfast.*

I was too busy being angry at God, wondering why He did all this to me. If God was so great, and He loved me so much, why did He keep ruining my life? Why did He put a little boy through all that pain? How is that love? I was throwing myself the world's biggest pity party and playing right into Satan's hands.

Instead of turning to God, I ran from Him. I did everything I knew was wrong. I cursed like a sailor, got drunk repeatedly, stole a car, sold drugs, lied, cheated, and went to strip clubs. I was out of control.

But somewhere in all that I craved the perfect life. I wanted the wife, the children, the dog, and a maid named Alice. I calmed down, asked God for forgiveness, and started on a quest to find a family. I met a girl and was married in five months. We had a baby boy nine months later. I was on my way. Her family loved me, and they even called me "Son." Could it get any better than this? All I needed was a dog and Alice.

The bottom fell out again. When our son was 18 months old, my wife told me she wanted to date other guys. Before I knew it she, my son, and my perfect family were gone. The vicious cycle started all over again. The depression, the drinking, and the thoughts of suicide consumed me.

My desires were all screwed up. I wanted the perfect family and I was going to make it happen. Me, Me, Me!

But Jesus says in Matthew 6:33; "*But seek first his kingdom and his righteousness, and all these things will be given to you as well.*" I needed to seek Jesus and His plan for my life but I was too stupid. I continued on the path to destruction. I was stuck in a cycle of sin and repentance, sin and repentance, never fully committing to Christ or surrendering my will to Him.

I started the process all over again. The pursuit of the perfect family, the need to belong, and to feel loved. I met another girl, did all the same things and ended up at the same place. Based on the definition of insanity we opened this book with, I was as crazy as they come.

Facing another divorce due to an unfaithful spouse sent my life in a downward spiral yet again. I blamed God. I was depressed. Thoughts of suicide crept in again. I couldn't go on knowing my dream, my desire, would never be fulfilled.

At twenty-eight I was alone and broken, right where God needed me.

6

Let's Make a Deal

JUST WHEN I THOUGHT THINGS could not get any worse, my mom suffered a heart attack. My brothers and I went to visit her in the hospital where we sat with her from 3:00 p.m. to 4:00 p.m. She seemed fine, so we left her sitting up in bed and ready to eat dinner. We told her we'd be back in an hour then stepped out to grab a bite to eat.

We returned to a chaotic nightmare, unable to get close to her room. A doctor greeted us in the hall and informed us a helicopter was on the way to fly her to Hahnemann Hospital in Philadelphia. Her heart was drowning in fluid. There was nothing more they could do. He suggested we say our goodbyes; she most likely wouldn't make it through the night.

The ringing in my ears was deafening. *She's only fifty. I can't lose her. God don't do this to me.* I begged Him. While waiting for the helicopter, I called Mom's church and asked them to pray for her. They assured me they would and put her on the prayer chain. I didn't know what a prayer chain was at the time, but it sounded good to me.

In the quiet of the waiting room I made a deal with God. I'm not advocating making deals with God but considering where I was at the time of my life, that is what I did. I remember telling God that if He let my mom live I would serve Him the rest of my life.

IN THE QUIET OF THE WAITING ROOM I MADE A DEAL WITH GOD.

The helicopter came and lifted off in a blinding snowstorm. I never felt more alone in my life.

The usual forty-five minute trip to the hospital took two hours due to the snowstorm. None of us spoke on the way. My brothers and I, estranged for so many years, were bound together again in tragedy. We arrived at the hospital and made our way to the floor she was on.

The elevator doors opened and we made a beeline for the nurse's station. We asked for my mother's room and the nurse asked us if we had heard the news. I know I don't have to tell you what was going through my mind. My life was stuck in a perpetual chasm of despair.

"We can't find anything wrong with her." My ears were failing me. What did she just say? The nurse repeated herself. They had done all the tests again and my mother had no fluid around her heart. They couldn't explain it, but I could. In that moment I knew exactly what was going on. And it was a miracle.

We rushed into my mother's room and unlike two hours earlier, when she had looked so frail, white, and scared, Mom was now sitting up in bed scolding us. "I told you not to drive all the way down here in this snowstorm." She was back. Mom was going to live.

That meant I was going to have to serve God or He was going to kill my mother; at least that's what I thought back then.

I started reading my Bible because if I had to serve God, He'd probably expect me to. I also started doing all the things I figured He'd want me to do—but something strange started happening. As I read His words, something inside me started to come to life. I began to want to pray and read the Bible, not because I felt I had to, but because I truly wanted to. It filled up in me something I'd been missing my whole life.

My earthly father died when I was nineteen years old, but I now knew my heavenly Father loved me, cared about me and wanted me. What else could I ask for?

I started attending my mom's church, which is where I met that long-haired guy named Jim. God was orchestrating things, and I was ready.

7

When a Door Closes

I HADN'T A CLUE HOW BIG 252 *Underground* would become considering its humble beginning in our 12 x 15 living room. But God did.

After returning from a missions trip to Belize, where I had a chance to share the gospel with a group of young people, something began to stir in me. The teens hadn't felt threatened by us and I had the best week of my life seeing many teens come to Christ. Something big was about to happen, but I didn't know what. Up until this point in my Christian walk I had struggled with waiting for God's response. There was too much noise in my life to hear His still small voice.

God was about to change that. Since He hadn't succeeded in getting through to me, He decided to slow me down. When the plane landed in Philadelphia, my head was pounding and I was burning up. I figured I just needed some rest and went home. It had been a hectic week spent sweating in the jungles of Belize.

Seven days later my fever was still 104. I had not eaten or had anything to drink in four days. I awoke on a Sunday morning after a relatively sleepless night, sure I was dying. My wife thought I was exaggerating because I have a slight tendency to do that when I am ill. I told her I could feel death was close. I could feel my body shutting down. They rushed me to the ER and my fever was 105. I guess that's bad because when the doctor took a look at the thermometer, things got a little crazy.

I TOLD HER I COULD FEEL DEATH WAS CLOSE.

The doctor informed us that I was extremely dehydrated and without immediate intervention, I would be dead in 24 to 48 hours. They admitted me to the ICU and quarantined me, unsure what I had contracted in the jungle. I eventually developed pneumonia. I was in the hospital, stuck in bed for seven days, with a lot of time to pray and nothing to do but listen. God healed me and I left the hospital.

I now felt God directing me to a ministry geared toward unchurched teenagers. By this time, I had been a member at my mother's church for five years so I assumed the ministry would be something done through that church. But once again, God had other plans.

The type of edgy ministry God was calling me into would not materialize in a traditional church setting. It didn't fit into the mold. Not every ministry has to be done through the church, but I couldn't see that at the time. I was young and passionate and wanted to forge ahead, but the pastor of the church knew better. He believed in the type of ministry I wanted to do, but he was smart enough to know that it would not flourish in that environment. I was disheartened because I believed I didn't have what it took to start a parachurch organization alone.

I parted ways with the church and prayed for wisdom. I spent two days sitting at a makeshift desk in my laundry room. and praying and listening for God's plan. I had no idea what was to come or what would be expected of me.

By Sunday night *252 Underground* was born. The name comes from Luke 2:52; *AND JESUS GREW IN WISDOM AND STATURE, AND IN FAVOR WITH GOD AND MAN*.

I thought this was appropriate because this verse covers the time when Jesus was twelve years old in the temple and the start of His public ministry at the age of thirty. The "Underground" in our name has two meanings. First, I figured the teens would find it cool; and second, I knew we'd have to go "underground" to meet them on their turf. We would use a backdoor approach to a relationship with Christ. Because there is a wall between the youth of today and the traditional church, *252 Underground* became a door bridging the two.

I printed out some postcards on my computer, hit the streets of Lansdale, and passed out the cards to teens hanging out on the street. The card promised video games, food, and fun every Friday night at my house.

I stapled black fabric and white Christmas lights to our 12 x 15 living room ceiling (God bless my wife). I rented a stereo system that had speakers as tall as me. We rented TVs, a Playstation®, and XBox game consoles, and lined them up on my porch (also wrapped in white Christmas lights). We went to Costco and bought enough candy for three Halloweens. We bought soda and French fries, mozzarella sticks and chicken fingers, along with a new fryer.

We got everything ready, but now I wondered if anyone would show. At six o'clock I saw a few kids making their way down our little street. I was excited and nervous all at the same time. This could work. That first night we had fifteen kids. They loved it! We were off to building friendships. The night ended with promise and renewed vigor. God called, I answered and He delivered. Wow, it was just like in the Bible.

One of the kids that came out was a boy T.R. He was one of the boys I told you about earlier who showed up on that Saturday night and asked me to pray for his friend whose father had killed himself. He had a blast. He didn't want to leave when it was over. He returned the second week with a friend named B. They both had a great time, and T.R. ate more mozzarella cheese sticks then I thought was possible.

The third week he shared with me that his father was a violent alcoholic and abused him. His mother had burned him with cigarettes as a baby. He had terrible scars from his hands to his elbows. I felt for him—I could relate to being abused.

The next night was a Saturday, the night the three young boys showed up on my doorstep. So after leading these three young men to Christ, I knew in my heart this was the beginning of something bigger than me. God was growing something in me that I knew would change the course of my life.

I had been comfortable in my church and hadn't wanted to leave, but God wanted to push me outside of my comfort zone. Sometimes He has to do that. He may be asking that of you. What if I hadn't followed God's vision? What if I had never left that church to pursue these kids on the fringes of society? You know what they say about when a door closes...

8

L o v e ' s   t h e   O n l y   R u l e

OUR GOAL AT 252 UNDERGROUND is not to get a bunch of kids to raise their hands and say a prayer. Wham, bam, you're saved. This method does not create true disciples or mean a teen has truly understood what it means to be a Christian. To me all it creates is a false conversion. Many have said a prayer to avoid hell, but it has no lasting impact on their life. They produce no fruit. They have essentially purchased fire insurance. There is no evidence that the Holy Spirit is alive in them. They continue as if nothing has changed, believing they are heaven bound because of that little prayer. The Bible, in fact, never mentions this prayer of salvation. A transformed life is the result and proof of salvation in biblical accounts.

Let's look at this:

Jesus entered Jericho and was passing through. A man was there by the name of Zacchaeus; he was a chief tax collector and was wealthy. He wanted to see who Jesus was, but because he was short he could not see over the crowd. So he ran ahead and claimed a sycamore-fig tree to see him, since Jesus was coming that way.

When Jesus reached the spot, he looked up and said to him, "Zacchaeus, come down immediately. I must stay at your house today." So he came down at once and welcomed him gladly.

All the people saw this and began to mutter, "He has gone to be the guest of a sinner."

But Zacchaeus stood up and said to the Lord, "Look, Lord! Here and now I give half of my possessions to the poor, and if I have cheated anybody out of anything, I will pay back four times the amount."

Jesus said to him, "Today salvation has come to this house, because this man, too, is a son of Abraham. For the Son of Man came to seek and to save the lost."

—Luke 19:1-19

Zacchaeus was curious about this Jesus he had heard so much about so he climbed up a tree to get a better look. Jesus spotted Zacchaeus and told him to come down at once because He wa coming to his house. Jesus called and Zacchaeus came without hesitation. The religious people complained that Jesus was associating with sinners (this could fill a book as well), but Jesus ignored them. After spending some time with Jesus, Zacchaeus stood up and said, "I give half my possessions to the poor, and if I have cheated anybody out of anything—as a tax collector this was almost certainly an understatement—I will pay them back four times the amount."

Jesus said to him, "Today salvation has come to this house, because this man, too, is a son of Abraham. For the Son of Man came to seek and to save what was lost."

There can be no transformation apart from Christ doing the work inside the man, woman, or teen. Every aspect of *252 Underground* is designed to produce transformed lives for Christ.

> THERE CAN BE NO TRANSFORMATION APART FROM CHRIST DOING THE WORK INSIDE THE MAN, WOMAN. OR TEEN.

In all my years in youth ministry, I've never had lunch with a hardcore teen which resulted in him completely surrendering his life to Christ, and I don't beat myself up over this. I just keep pointing them to the love of God, to Jesus. That is the calling.

We don't know the back story of Zacchaeus, but we do know that when you're sitting across the table with the Savior of the world, things have a way of miraculously working out.

False conversions are easy to spot. These kids go to youth camp every year and find God. It's not hard because He's right where they left

Him last year. For two weeks, everyone is warm and fuzzy. All is well at Christian Church USA ... Then it's like it never happened. If you have been in youth ministry more than ten minutes you've seen this scenario or one like it.

This is why it's so important to build relationships and to pour into the lives of these young people daily. We live out our faith with the teens we minister to. We get them involved with helping the needy. We do service projects with them to help our communities, and cultivate the soil of their heart with the things of God before they become a follower of Christ.

We allow the Spirit to work in their heart and wait for the right time to harvest. Only the Spirit can cause growth. That is why traditional youth ministry methods don't last. They are manufactured to get a desired result, without the relational investment. There is no connection beyond the motivational speech with the canned metaphors and tear-jerking stories.

We know we are called to make disciples, but what exactly does that mean?

My definition of a disciple of Christ is someone who is head over heels in love with Christ—so in love they want to talk to Him every day.

Remember your first girlfriend or boyfriend, how you talked on the phone for hours about nothing, but it meant everything? You could not wait to see him or her, even though you'd just hung up the phone from talking with them.

That's how a true disciple of Christ feels about Him. Love is so very powerful; we look for ways to express our love and devotion. We don't need to be told how to treat those we love; we want them to be happy. If a husband truly loves his wife, I don't have to tell him not to cheat on her because he would never even dream of it. I would not have to tell him to kiss his wife or hug her, or tell her she is beautiful. He would do these things because he loves her. When you're in love, you don't need rules because love IS the rule.

When a teenager has a genuine encounter with the Spirit of God, a Damascus Road experience if you will, they can't help but produce fruit. You won't have to run around telling them not to do drugs or drink. You will not have to tell them not to get their girlfriend pregnant. You will not have to bottle feed them spiritual milk. When a teen experiences this love for Jesus, there is no need to post rules in our building because love's the only rule.

9

A Different Kind of Animal

I WANT TO STRESS THE importance of making the gospel relevant to today's youth. They need to understand how God's Word applies to them today.

If Jesus were speaking to us today, He would not be telling us parables about sheep and grapevines. His illustrations would include movies, books, and technology, because that's what we understand. He might reference Twitter or Snapchat or YouTube. I know this because Jesus was relevant. He spoke truth and used object lessons centered on everyday things. Why would He not do the same if He walked the earth today?

But remember, before we can start telling relevant parables to teenagers in our communities, we have to build relationships with them. This may sound difficult, but it is so much easier than you think. If you are sincere, it will be a natural process and will clear the way to present the gospel to the young people in your community.

I call it planting to reap. To see this process in action we need only to look at the farmer.

In anticipation the farmer starts out early in the season to prepare the ground, to soften it up to receive the seed he is going to plant. He then plants the seed. He comes back to water and nurture it onto maturity. After a period of time, his hard work and devotion pays off. He reaps a great harvest.

Relational evangelism is exactly like this. We take time to develop a meaningful relationship/friendship. One built on sincerity and trust. (*Preparing the soil to accept the seed*).

As we develop these relationships we earn the right to be heard. We can now share our testimony or the gospel with them. (*Plant the seed*).

These friends are not going to sprout into new Christians overnight. We need to continue building the relationship; strengthening them in the knowledge of Christ and His love with continual encouragement. (*Watering the Seed*).

As this progresses there is a great probability they will make a decision to follow Christ. (*The Harvest*). Man plants the seed, God brings the harvest.

We then teach them to duplicate the process. We do this every day, always anticipating a harvest or teaching others how to plant. (*Making Disciples*).

Christians make evangelism complicated and too often we disqualify ourselves because we don't know enough. It's best left to the professionals, isn't it? What you fail to realize is that professional evangelists can come across like used car salesmen to the unchurched crowd and we all know how we feel about those guys. The other disadvantage is they are usually hired to speak at your church, do not have a relationship with these teens, or speak at a place where the teens are hanging out.

We are the hands and feet of Jesus, and we might be the first and only encounter someone outside the church has with Jesus.

> WE ARE THE HANDS AND FEET OF JESUS, AND YOU MIGHT BE THE FIRST AND ONLY ENCOUNTER SOMEONE OUTSIDE THE CHURCH HAS WITH JESUS.

The first and most important step of the relational process is preparing the soil. If we don't get this right we won't get to the other steps. Jesus illustrates the importance of the soil in the parable of the farmer. He speaks about four kinds of soil: the rocks, the shallow soil, the soil choked with weeds, and good soil. Only one type of soil produces a harvest: the prepared ground that is ready to receive the seed.

Making sure we facilitate the proper preparation of the soil to receive the seed is paramount to success. We have our work cut out for us as a church because in the minds of most teenagers, going to church is like going to the dentist. They will fight you tooth and nail. On the other hand, if you said you were going to Applebee's they would be in the car before you and begging to bring some of their friends along.

We need to create an environment that teens want to come to and bring their friends. Accomplish that and the battle is half won.

In 1 Corinthians 9:19-23, Paul explains his way of preparing the soil. He said in verse 22 "*To the weak I became weak, to win the weak. I have become all things to all people so that by all possible means I might save some.*" He essentially put himself in their place. He walked in their shoes and felt what they felt. He found common ground.

G a m e   P l a n

Here is my simple blueprint for relational evangelism. It has been tested and has proven successful, resulting in over 110 teens accepting Christ in the last five years.

1) Initiate Contact

Reach out to teens. They are not going to come to us. They don't know their need for Christ because Satan has blinded them. They will be less guarded on their own turf.

2) Establish Common Ground

Find something you have in common. This could be video games, music, movies, or social networking. Be genuine. Remember we are not used car salesmen. If you don't know anything about video games, don't act like you do. Teens can spot a poser and you will lose credibility.

3) Listen

I'm sure you've heard the phrase: God gave us two ears and one mouth for a reason. He wants us to listen twice as much as we speak, so make sure you really listen when they open up to you. Don't be plotting and planning your next move—save that for the chess game. Don't be thinking about how you're going to force feed the gospel to them. The Spirit will lead you in this area.

4) Arouse Interest

If you've followed step 3 and were really listening, then you probably heard some things about their lives that they are unhappy about. Could be a job, their family, finances, a relationship, or their future. Any one of these things are door openers to a relationship. A door opener allows those on the outside to come inside. This, after all, is what we are trying to accomplish.

As you listen, find something you can personally relate to and share with them how you handled the situation. When you are sincere and show you genuinely care about what they care about, they will see you as an ally. They will see you as a normal person not a Bible-thumping nut case. You will be on your way to building a friendship and trust. Both of these will allow you to speak into their lives.

5) Don't Judge

As you listen to what they share, you will hear things about their lives that you don't agree with or approve of. Don't give in to the urge to tell them all the things they are doing wrong. This is key, but it is often the point in the relationship where we blow it. It's hard to recover from.

In order to love people unconditionally, we must understand the difference between acceptance and approval. We are called to accept and love unbelievers without approving of their lifestyles.

We need to give unbelievers some slack. The Holy Spirit will convict them just like He convicts you and me. Remember we cannot expect unbelievers to act like believers until they are. Paul says in Romans 8:9 that it's impossible because they don't have the Holy Spirit. Start with where people are and guide them to where Christ wants them to be.

6) Let Love Motivate You

We should be a beacon of hope, a lifeboat in the raging sea that is their lives. You can provide safety, a haven in the storm, but if love is not the motivation you can make the problem worse.

Picture this. You are lost at sea after your boat has capsized in a storm. Immense waves crash over you, and you flail in fear of drowning. You're tired, ready to give up when you spot a lifeboat. Relieved, you muster the strength to swim towards it. On sheer adrenaline you reach the boat, grab the side and using every bit of strength you can muster, you pull yourself up. As you are ready to drag yourself into the safety of the boat, though, you realize in horror that the boat is filled with deadly king cobras, rattlesnakes, vipers, and scorpions. Despair replaces hope. What should have been salvation reveals itself to be a false promise. Would you continue crawling into the boat, or thrust yourself back into the raging sea? I'm betting you might very well take your chances with the raging sea—you'd rather face drowning than get into that boat.

Unfortunately much of the church is like that lifeboat—filled with venomous judgmental hypocrites. That is why so many unbelievers choose to take their chances with the world. The church is judgmental; the corner bar seems safer and more like a family.

Our calling and purpose is to be a light in the darkness to guide those that are lost to Christ. Let love be our aim.

7) Take Them Only as Far as They are Ready to Go

Tell them enough truth to make them hungry for more. Get them asking questions. We do not have to be afraid of questions—the answer is always Jesus. Too often when we get the opportunity, we spend six minutes "witnessing" by giving them an overview of Genesis through Revelation without taking a breath. When we realize we are about to pass out, we grab some oxygen and exhale, saying, "just repeat this prayer after me so we can make sure if you step out on the sidewalk and an 18 wheeler jumps the curb and squashes you, you won't go to hell, 'kay?"

IF THIS GUY'S GOING TO HEAVEN, MAYBE HELL AIN'T SO BAD.

All the while their eyes are bugged out of their head and they're looking for an escape—any reason to get away from you. They may even be thinking *If this guy's going to heaven, maybe hell ain't so bad.*

Don't be a freak, be relatable. Jesus was relatable, so follow His example.

8) Accept Others Where They are At

Acceptance is different from approval. Jesus knew the lifestyle of the woman at the well but did not condemn her for it.

Think about the kind of person you like to hang out with and be that person, but more importantly, think about the person you can't stand and don't be that one.

9) Communicate Directly and Simply

Don't confuse people. Just because you know everything in the Bible and understand the Trinity completely AND did your dissertation on Revelation, this does not mean they will get it. Remember it took you years to obtain the biblical knowledge you now wield like a sawed-off shotgun. Slow down. Don't run, and don't drag them. WALK with them.

Use simple terms they can understand and relate to. And never start in Revelation; even Bible scholars struggle with this book. Save that discussion for much later.

10) Don't Prejudge or Pre-Qualify

We are called to be witnesses not judges. Christ died that none should perish. Salvation is not just for the folks with short hair and dress suits and shiny shoes with six figure incomes.

Jesus came for the dirty homeless guy with the missing teeth. He came for the drug addict, the drunk, the foul mouthed disrespectful punk teenager, the prostitute... I think you get the picture.

Jesus called us to be fishers of men. That's it, period. Not cleaners of fish. Jesus is the hook, so put some relevant bait on and dangle the line in the sea of mankind—Jesus will catch them. He will clean them. That's not our job. Our job is simply to get the bait in front of the fish.

11) Bait, Bait, Bait

Use the right kind of bait for the fish you want to catch. Don't use old hymns to reach teens, or death metal music to reach the seniors.

If you went fishing and forgot your bait at home, your big nasty pointy sharp hook thingy wouldn't attract fish.

Love is the best bait. Don't go fishing for men without the love of Jesus—it only repels them.

10

Main Street, Not Easy Street

USING THE TECHNIQUES in the last chapter we quickly grew out of our living room and needed to find a larger location. Up to this point we had not sought any outside financial help. My wife and I painted houses during the day and paid for everything from those funds. God blessed us with plenty of work so we could operate *252 Underground.*

I had hoped the local churches, after seeing what we were doing, would be eager to support us, but that was not the case. Churches have so many obligations and never enough funds to cover them, and I guess the thought of supporting a fledgling parachurch organization was the last thing on their agenda. I was on my own. I figured God had me in this ministry and He saw that we needed more room, so I went looking for a storefront to rent in Lansdale. I prayed about a new location but didn't really wait for God to speak.

What eventually became obvious, but at the time somehow escaped me, was the fact that I got ahead of God. I'm going to share this experience with you because just as the Bible shares the good and bad things with us, I want you to know the mistakes I made so you can learn from them if you face similar situations. In the end, God worked all things out, but the journey is worth documenting.

Previously I shared with you that before I put my faith and trust in Jesus, I was continually trying to have the perfect family. The key word here is I. I was doing it. I was pursuing a wife. I was going to make it happen. My way. I. I. I. Me. Me. Me.

But as God molded me and shaped me to His will for my life, I stumbled across Matthew 6:33:

> *But seek first his kingdom and his righteousness, and all these things will be given to you as well.*

What were these things that would be given to me? The desires of my heart—if my desires were the same as God's for my life.

When I realized I had put having the perfect family above God and had made that an idol, I immediately vowed I would put God first in every area of my life. I would no longer seek a soul mate for myself. After all, I had a poor but proven track record with my first three marriages ending in FAILURE.

Trust me, hindsight is 20/20. The lifelong mission God was going to call me to would not have come to fruition with the women that I sought out and married, but when I put my faith and trust in Jesus He brought the right woman right to my front door.

God is faithful when we seek him first.

I was a single father raising two boys, ages 2 and 3, when my doorbell rang one night at 10:00 p.m. When I answered the door a young man from my youth ministry stood there. He informed me that his mother had locked him out of the house and he had nowhere to go. Could he stay the night at my house?

As we talked I learned his 18th birthday was a week away, but there would be no party because he had nowhere to have it.

"Have it here at my house," I told him, and then jokingly added, "just bring me a date." The following Saturday we held the party and he showed up with a "date" for me. She was eighteen and I was thirty-one. Not going to happen. I did however ask her if she had any older sisters.

Yes, she had two.

"Do you happen to have any pictures of them on you?"

She retrieved two photos from her wallet which I then looked at. They were both beautiful women. I pointed to one of them and said, "I'll take that one."

"That is my sister Stephanie."

The next night Stephanie showed up at my house to meet me. To make an amazingly long and beautiful story fit within the context of this book, Stephanie and I have been married eighteen years.

> I POINTED TO ONE OF THEM AND SAID, "I'LL TAKE THAT ONE." SHE SAID, "THAT IS MY SISTER STEPHANIE."

I know without question God brought her to me. Everyone who knows of my ministry says, "Man. You are lucky you married Stephanie, because no one else would let you do the things you do."

They are 1,000 percent correct. Stephanie has been my rock, and she has my back. She has put up with everything, even allowing me to move seven homeless people into our home for five months. Before we had a building, she allowed me to run a youth ministry out of our home, and she cooked and cleaned up for hundreds of kids. She has stood with me when we were broke because I spent all our money on hurting teenagers.

I can testify, God gives you what you need when you need it. Give your desires to God and let him take care of things. He knows what you need. He truly gave me the desires of my heart. I could not have picked a better, more suited helpmate and wife than Stephanie. If it were not for Stephanie, you would not be reading this book because I would have no story to tell.

Now back to our regularly scheduled program ...

My wife and I, along with our three-year-old son, Christian, visited Main Street to check out a few empty storefronts. We found a parking space and had planned on heading west on Main but Christian ran east and I gave chase. He stopped in front of an empty storefront that used to be a dance studio. There was a rent sign in the window. I called the number and left a message. We proceeded west on Main and looked at two locations, both less than 1,000 square feet. Both wanted $2500 per month in rent as well as $7500 up front to move in. I would not be able to afford either of these and, even if I could, neither of them was large enough for what I had in mind. My excitement about the future possibilities quickly faded. We stopped for lunch and while we were eating I got a call from the first place—the one my son ran to.

Before he told me the price of the rent I told him upfront that I was sure there was no way I could afford to rent his place. He asked me what I wanted to do with the location, and I shared with him the vision God gave me. He told me he wanted to speak to his wife that night and he would tell me the next day when we looked at the space how much the rent would be. I didn't get my hopes up. The space was 1,500 square feet and located in a prime retail location. I had seen two locations less than 1,000 square feet going for $2500. I could only imagine what this guy was going to want.

We went to look at the building the next day and though it was just a shell, I saw tons of potential. The location was perfect. It was located at the busiest intersection in Lansdale with 30,000 cars a day passing by. The junior high school with over 1,500 students was four blocks away.

Joe, the owner, told me that he and his wife had discussed it and they would rent me the location for $1,100 per month—the cost of the mortgage. They were willing to forgo earning a profit on the space in order to help me in my ministry. We could move in for only $2,200, the first month's rent and one month security deposit. It seemed possible we might be able to rent this location after all.

Joe was gracious and agreed to hold the building for one week to give me a chance to raise the funds. I set out extremely optimistic, believing people would throw money at this much-needed ministry. Once again, I was wrong. In six days, I'd only raised $1,200 and it looked as if I would not meet our goal or Joe's deadline. But on the last day, day seven, we received a gift for $1,000. We were going to get our place on Main Street after all!

I signed the lease and could not wait to get started on a design I'd thought of to remodel the inside. A day or two in, though, it occurred to me that this ministry was God's and I hadn't consulted Him on the design. That night, I decided to ask God to reveal His plan for the building to me.

I went to bed at 2:00 a.m. and immediately dozed off. In a vivid dream, I opened the front door of the building and saw a completed interior space, perfect for *Underground 252*. God had revealed His design to me. I jumped out of bed and woke my wife, sharing with her what God had showed me in my dream. I then drew detailed pictures of the interior I had seen. Over the next month, some items were donated for the design that matched my rendering of the dream perfectly.

I thought people would line up to help with the building project and again I was disappointed. A thirty day goal to open turned into ninety days. I spent days working on the project alone and grew discouraged. I couldn't afford all the materials needed for the construction of the interior.

> I THOUGHT PEOPLE WOULD LINE UP TO HELP WITH THE BUILDING PROJECT AND AGAIN I WAS DISAPPOINTED.

I contacted the local newspaper and they ran a story on what we were doing. I was sure the newspaper article would generate tons of interest resulting in people wanting to help with the building as well as the finances, but only three people called. Two of them were contractors who succeeded in getting some donated materials and we built a large portion of the interior in a short amount of time. I was enthusiastic about our progress until the volunteers had to pull off the job. Once again I was alone, wondering if we would ever open.

While leading a youth Bible study one night at a local church, I shared with the kids what I was doing and said if anyone wanted to help they could come by. The next day Byron, a sixteen-year-old boy, showed up. He told me he was homeschooled and his mom said he could take a two week break to help me. Byron and I had the greatest time together putting in twelve- to fifteen-hour days—times we both will never forget.

As we were nearing completion and our grand opening was less than a week away, I ran out of money for supplies. Once again I was discouraged. But that night Byron showed up with his family and handed me an envelope filled with money that he and his sister had earned. I was moved beyond words and so blessed by their generosity, but I could tell they were more blessed. I've learned that's how this family is; they give and give, expecting nothing in return.

A week prior to opening night, we printed three hundred ads that looked like concert tickets and distributed them to kids as they passed our location. One thing I learned over the years—kids don't plan far in advance and usually go with the last thing they were invited to, so make a note of that. We were not sure how many would actually come but we had hyped up the curiosity by covering the windows and just hanging a sign that said, *252 IS COMING*, nothing more. We finished with the building and cleanup thirty minutes before we opened the doors.

Twenty adults from a local church showed up to help and brought their young children. Not good. The little kids ran around screaming. As the teens piled in, the screaming kids tied up the video games and the adults stood around watching the teens as they entered. The teens left as quickly as they came. In my experience, teens want to get away from their younger siblings, and they do not want to hang out with adults watching their every move.

I quickly asked the parents with children to leave and the few adults that had stayed removed their coats and relaxed a bit. One teen serving as lookout, returned shortly with a bunch of others and in no time we had 104 teenagers hanging out having a good time. I tell you all this so that you don't make these same mistakes.

After that first night, my help disappeared—all but Byron. We were left with a ton of teenagers every Friday night, but no volunteers, and no money for food and drinks.

To say it was a constant struggle would be an understatement. We closed our doors twice due to lack of funding.

It took me two and half years to realize I had gotten ahead of God. And that realization came when I read Nehemiah.

Like me, Nehemiah had a vision, but that is where the similarities end. Though I believe God intended us to be where we are today, He had a different time frame in mind than I did. I chose to rush ahead, but His timing is always right.

Nehemiah has a lot to teach us about how he handled his vision and made it a reality; it's textbook wisdom. Read Nehemiah for yourself. It can help you avoid a lot of the pitfalls that caused me so much trouble.

Nehemiah received a vision from God concerning the broken-down condition of the walls around Jerusalem. Unlike me though he didn't rush headlong into fulfilling it. He prayed about it for four months. I think I prayed for four minutes.

Nehemiah didn't sneak off in the middle of the night and go to the stone depot to purchase a little bit of stone with his available funds. He didn't start building the wall himself. He waited. Andy Stanley says it best in his great book, *Visioneering*: "Nehemiah knew what so many of us have a hard time remembering, (especially me). What could be and should be, can't be until God is ready for it to be."

> WHAT COULD BE AND SHOULD BE, CAN'T BE UNTIL GOD IS READY FOR IT TO BE.

Boy, I wish I had read that sooner. I jumped out of the gate too early and faced failure and disillusionment. Discouraged, I even questioned God. Yet, there came a time when everything started to fall into place. People got on board and money started rolling in.

That's what happened in Nehemiah's case. In the four months he prayed, God was working. He orchestrated events that allowed Nehemiah to find favor in the eyes of the king, moved people's hearts to provide materials and permits, all while working in Nehemiah's heart as well.

Nehemiah knew what he was up against in his plan to rebuild the wall. Jerusalem had been without walls for 120 years. The people didn't seem to care. They probably felt the walls were unnecessary—not to mention, the surrounding enemies would certainly be opposed to Jerusalem fortifying itself.

What if, in the face of all those obstacles, Nehemiah ran off that very night and started to work on fulfilling the vision God placed in his heart? What would have been the outcome? He would have failed miserably even though God wanted the walls rebuilt. And when he failed, people would have said, "I guess it just wasn't God's will. It just wasn't meant to be."

I know about this because those are the things people said to me as I faced one failure after another. God did want it to be. He gave me the vision. He called me into the ministry. But I was working His vision on my time line, not His.

Make sure that whatever you do for God, you do on His timeline. And remember, you can never pray too much. In fact, gather together a team of dedicated prayer warriors who share the same vision and heart for young people to pray with you.

I also recommend you read Andy Stanley's book, *Visioneering*[1], before you go forward with any vision you may have. The wisdom in his book proved invaluable to me and would have saved me much time and disappointment.

---

1. Stanley, Andy. Visioneering: Your Guide for Discovering and Maintaining Your Personal Vision. 2005, Multnomah.

"

Better than Drugs

GETTING THE TEENS INVOLVED in service projects is part of our discipling pre-conversion process, and neighborhood projects are never in short supply.

One of the things I like to do is help the victims of house fires. I might read an article in our local paper about one, or see smoke and walk or drive to the scene. I then record it with my phone so I can later show the teens. With the popularity of YouTube, they are stimulated through video.

The following is one instance where we were able to help a family that lost everything in a fire.

On a blistery January afternoon we saw smoke, so one of my leaders and I drove to where the firefighters were trying to save the home. It was a total loss. After recording their efforts and the ravaged home, I immediately began my investigation. Who lived there? Did they have insurance? What were their immediate needs?

Within twenty-four hours I put a team of young people together, coupled with some older guys from our newly formed college ministry. These college guys had been dipping their toes in the gospel but had yet to make a decision to follow Christ.

We helped the family find a new home to rent. I, along with my team of young people, custom painted the entire interior with colors chosen by the mom. We got people to donate furniture. We bought them new appliances. We stocked the cabinets with food. We shopped clearance stores and decorated the house with new curtains, plants, pictuers, and knick-knacks to make it a home. We bought new toys for the two little boys and a new laptop for the seventeen-year-old. All this came from monies that were donated.

We were able to accomplish all of this in nine days. Just this band of young people united in a common purpose.

We called it extreme home makeover, God edition. We unveiled the home to the family and they could not stop crying. They thanked us and Joe, one of the college guys, fell to his knees and thanked the family for allowing him to do this. He said it was better than any drug he had ever done. He could not wait to do something like this again. In fact everyone involved had the same sentiment.

These young people got to see a powerful move of God before they were even on His team. It was better than any sermon I could have given. They lived it. It was faith in action and it changed every one of them.

They had been hearing of miraculous stories from the Bible, but they were just stories to them. Old stories. But, there was no mistaking the miraculous provision of God and what He did through a band of willing misfit youths. They now had their own story to tell, and it was powerful.

Our local paper was so blown away by what we had accomplished they ran a front page story. These young people who had once been addicted to drugs became addicted to serving others.

Get young people involved, even if they are not on the team yet. Jesus called the disciples to follow Him and He put them to work before they really even knew who He was. There is no better way to preach the gospel message than to live it out in front of them and let them have a part in it.

Everyone involved in that project accepted Christ since then, and Joe is now in College getting his degree in ministry.

12

Building a Team

NO MAN IS AN ISLAND. If you want to be successful reaching the youth in your community, you need to put together a team of dedicated leaders to help you accomplish the vision God has given you.

This is an area where I struggled at first, but God has graciously pulled me through and taught me invaluable lessons from my experiences.

Early on, I would take anyone with a pulse willing to help, but that often proved more detrimental to the ministry than helpful. I learned that not everyone with a heart for missions is called to reaching unchurched teens.

Some mission-minded people partnered with us only to find out they were better suited to reaching seniors, as in over sixty-five.

As our ministry took off, we were approached by a multitude of mission-minded people inspired after reading about *252 Underground* in the paper. They wanted to get involved. These well-meaning helpers often criticized the teens for smoking or wearing their pants too low, thought their music was of the devil, and their purple hair and Mohawks were ridiculous. The list of criticisms was endless.

Some volunteers preached the gospel on a teen's first visit, never thinking of the fact they hadn't built a relationship with them that earned them the right to be heard. This caused a lot of ill feelings and alienated some of the teens we were trying to reach.

Maybe you'll relate to this analogy:

You meet me and think I'm a pretty cool dude. We start to hang out and I show you I care about you by meeting a few of your needs. One day I invite you to my house for dinner. You'd come expecting to have a great night, right? What would you do if my wife came into the dining room as you were sitting down to eat and began to point out all your faults? What if she looked down on you in self-righteous contempt and made you feel worthless?

Would you come back for dinner the following week if I invited you? Stupid question. You probably wouldn't come even if you were starving. You'd probably wonder why I married my wife in the first place, and would most likely avoid me so as not to run into her again.

That's how the majority of the church, the bride of Christ, acts toward teens today. Teens actually like Jesus. He's cool. They just can't stand His bride and millions of adults feel the same.

TEENS ACTUALLY LIKE JESUS. HE'S COOL. THEY JUST CAN'T STAND HIS BRIDE.

Accepting the responsibility for our mistakes, I developed a training program designed to qualify our volunteers and integrate them into the ministries at *252 Underground.*

I now meet with potential helpers and share the vision, explain the difference between acceptance and approval, tell them what to expect, and give tips for how to handle certain situations. There is no "one size fits all" approach to fishing.

After these one on one's, if they feel compelled to continue the process, they are brought in as observers. We invite them out on a Wednesday night, which compared to Friday is tame.

Wednesday nights, the music is not as loud and the atmosphere is different. We give a faith-based message, and it's attended by kids who have been coming to the Friday night events for a while. We have developed relationships with these kids and have earned respect and the right to be heard.

Wednesday nights give us the opportunity to show these potential helpers we are gospel intentional and what we are doing is making an impact. If they enjoy themselves and agree with the way we teach the teens, we invite them back for a Friday night event.

Friday nights are always packed and a bit on the wild side. It's all about making that first contact. The music is loud and usually live. Lots of teens have bands and we allow them to play, so naturally they invite their friends.

Free hot meals, tons of candy, and gallons of soda help us build awesome relationships in a fun, safe environment. The most exciting part is never knowing who will walk in the door.

Hundreds of teens have asked why we do this for them. When they ask questions, it gives us the opportunity to respond. They are inviting us to share our faith with them without even realizing it.

Many teens cannot believe we are Christians. They say things like "you are too nice to us" or "Christians would never do this for us." We catch them off guard on their own turf and make a lasting impact.

Friday nights also allow teens who have given their hearts to Christ a comfortable way to invite their friends into their new-found faith community. They know we won't preach at their friends and their friends will love *252 Underground.*

Remember the reference I made earlier to Applebee's and how your kids are excited about it and want to take their friends along? Teens love to invite their friends to *252 Underground*, and that's half the battle.

It's a totally different response from trying to get teens to invite a friend to church.

If a potential helper still wants to be involved after witnessing a Friday night, we know they will make the long commitment.

We then put them in a position to serve the teens, either in the kitchen or at the video game counter. This gives the teens a chance to get to know them, and they in turn become familiar with the teens and learn their names. Teens are always surprised when they come back a second time and I know their name. They feel important and they are. This is a sentence you should highlight—*get good at remembering names.*

After a period of time, and as the teens accept this helper, they move into positions of mentoring and discipling the teens. You should put some sort of process in place to qualify helpers at this point as well.

Look for people who are willing to make a long-term commitment. If you have new leaders popping in and out every couple of months, it doesn't provide the stability these young people need—and it gets harder for them to open up to someone.

Ask for a minimum one-year commitment, although three years would be ideal.

When I founded *252 Underground*, the kids who were thirteen years old are now in their twenties. I've watched them grow from awkward teenagers into young men and women. I've helped them through their first dating relationships and helped some get their first job. I've walked with some through their parents' divorcing. I've seen some go off to college, and a few become parents.

I have a bond with them, and when I speak into their lives they listen because I've been there every step of the way. Do you get that? They listen because they know I love them. They trust me and know I only want the best for them.

You can't build a relationship this strong and meaningful if it is just a hobby you're into today, but maybe not tomorrow. Many church youth ministries are like this. All too often, a youth pastor is hired, and as they begin to build relationships and make plans with the kids, they get a better job offer and are gone.

The kids are crushed. Then the church hires another guy right out of seminary and he follows the same vicious cycle.

Too many see the position of youth pastor as a stepping-stone on the way to better things, and in its wake it leaves disheartened young people who lose faith in the church and ultimately God. We need to stop the damage now by placing appropriate honor on the position of a youth pastor because he/she lays the foundation for the church of tomorrow.

Don't miss this—without strong youth ministries raising teens into sold-out followers of Christ, there will be no adults in need of a senior pastor. You need only look at the condition of the American church today to know that I speak the truth.

Be committed or stay home. If this seems harsh, it's meant to be.

13

Lessons from The Master

A COUPLE YEARS AGO MY PILOT went out on my water heater. I had no idea how to relight it. I called my father-in-law but he was out of town. I do not like cold showers so something had to be done. I grabbed my toolbox and headed to the basement to try and light it.

Since I did not have a clue what I was doing, I was afraid I was going to blow up the house. The last thing I wanted to do was stick a match by an open gas line.

I took the cover off the big round bomb to expose the little pilot thingy and aimed my flashlight on it. Unfortunately this did not shed any light on the situation. I followed the instructions printed on the

I IMAGINED THE GAS BUILDING UP AND HOW I WOULD MEET JESUS THE NEXT TIME I LIT THE MATCH.

water heater; turned the gas switch, pushed a button, and put the match in the opening. I imagined the gas building up and how I would meet Jesus the next time I lit the match.

Suddenly I had the idea to stop using my phone as a flashlight and use it to Google, "How to light a water heater pilot." Sure enough there was a YouTube video instructing me how to light the very same model I had. I watched the video and lit the pilot on the first try.

I watched the expert and was able to duplicate what he had done. My grandfather's words rang true, "If you want to make a million dollars, go find a millionaire and ask him how he did it." Or in my case, "if you want to light a water heater …"

My grandfather was a smart man and his advice was sound. That's the reason I went straight to the New Testament when I wanted to learn how to reach teens for Jesus. Of course you can reach people of all ages— but remember I was called to youth ministry so just go with it.

When you're looking for examples on reaching people for Jesus there is no one better than…well Jesus.

In John 12:32 Jesus said; *And I, when I am lifted up from the earth, will draw all people to myself."*

As you read the account of Jesus' earthly ministry in the Gospels you see a pattern emerge in the methods He used to reach the lost. Jesus is the expert in the field of relational evangelism. He drew bigger crowds than Wal-Mart on black Friday, every day of the week.

Although there are many encounters between Jesus and lost people, He followed three simple steps every time:

He loved them.

He met their needs.

He taught them in interesting ways.

These same three steps still attract people to Him today.

Let's take a look at each step.

He Loved Them

Jesus loved people and had compassion on them. Matthew 9:36 says:

When he saw the crowds, he had compassion on them, because they were harassed and helpless, like sheep without a shepherd.

Loving unbelievers the way Jesus did is the most overlooked but most effective key to reaching people with the gospel message. Without His passion and a burden for the lost we will be unwilling to make the sacrifices necessary to reach them.

The right climate for growing a healthy youth ministry is an atmosphere of acceptance and love. Like my friend Jim, you must have the mindset; "we're going to love you no matter who you are, what you look like, or what you've done."

Remember, we talked about the difference between acceptance and approval. We are called to love unbelievers unconditionally without approving of their lifestyles.

That's what Jesus does for us. We are just following His example.

THE CATALYST FOR ANY MINISTRY NEEDS TO BE LOVE.

I read that growing churches love and loving churches grow. My experience has proven this to be true. The catalyst for any ministry needs to be love. Ministering out of duty and obligation will only produce mediocre results that don't last.

I talk a lot about love in this book because when people know you love them, they listen to you. An open ear can lead to an open heart.

He Met Their Needs

Great crowds came to him, bringing the lame, the blind, the crippled, and the mute and many others, and laid them at his feet; and he healed them. The people were amazed when they saw the mute speaking, the crippled made well, the lame walking and the blind seeing. And they praised the God of Israel.

—Matthew 15:30-31

Meeting someone's needs tends to make them very receptive to your message because there is action to your faith. They see you really believe what you are saying because you practice what you preach.

In situations where I was able to meet someone's need, it opened the door for me to share the gospel message.

Remember the family that lost everything in the fire and how the young people were transformed through that ordeal? We were the hands and feet of Jesus to them. And when we prayed with them, they wept. The generosity and outpouring of love from a group of people they never met softened their hearts to the gospel.

I've also met some tough looking, foul-mouthed teens that broke down in tears when I bought them a much needed pair of sneakers or just spent time with them when they were hurting.

Once delivering groceries to a teen's family in need, a father I'd just met shared his situation with me through tears and asked me to pray for his family.

We met a single mom whose kids came to *252 Underground*—she had no Christmas presents for her kids. We purchased gifts for her to give to them. We also provided Christmas dinner and paid some past-due bills. Then we went with a group to paint her living room and fix some things around her house.

We invested a year in this woman and her family, even though she was not a believer. Her heart melted and the Holy Spirit stirred her to repentance. I had the privilege to baptize her, and she is now in a church family serving the Lord and helping others.

I could fill this book with stories just like these, but I'd rather equip you to make your own.

Too often we Christians are known more for what we stand against than who we stand for. When you stand for Jesus, the needs of all men and women matter.

He Taught Them in Interesting and Practical Ways

Jesus spoke all these things to the crowd in parables; he did not say anything to them without using a parable.

—Matthew 13:34

Wikipedia defines a parable as a succinct story, in prose or verse, which illustrates one or more principles, or lessons.

Everyone loves a good story. We tend to remember a story long after we've forgotten the facts. I use parables when teaching the teens at *252 Underground*. I even modernize parables and stories from the Bible. I always share the original as well but I find when I teach in the context of "now," they understand and grasp the principle of the message better.

Be a storyteller. Look for teachable moments in everyday life and create a story that will capture their attention and make learning fun.

You only need to look at the story of Nathan and David in the Old Testament to understand the value in a story.

BE A STORYTELLER.

David had committed adultery and what amounted to murder to cover it up. He was the king so who was going to challenge him, right?

Along comes Nathan. Now Nathan can call the king out on his sin and risk being put to death when David becomes defensive, or he can reveal the extent of David's sin through a poignant story. Nathan wisely chooses the latter.

Let's look at the story.

> The LORD sent Nathan to David. When he came to him, he said, "There were two men in a certain town, one rich and the other poor. The rich man had a very large number of sheep and cattle, but the poor man had nothing except one little ewe lamb he had bought. He raised it, and it grew up with him and his children. It shared his food, drank from his cup and even slept in his arms. It was like a daughter to him.
>
> Now a traveler came to the rich man, but the rich man refrained from taking one of his own sheep or cattle to prepare

a meal for the traveler who had come to him. Instead, he took the ewe lamb that belonged to the poor man and prepared it for the one who had come to him."

David burned with anger against the man and said to Nathan, "As surely as the LORD lives, this man who did this must die! He must pay for that lamb four times over, because he did such a thing and had no pity."

Then Nathan said to David, "You're that man!"

—2 Samuel 12:1-5.

Talk about a gut punch. This powerful story brought about David's repentance and ultimate restoration.

I had the opportunity, when confronting a leader in our ministry who had sinned, to use this same approach. When the man became angry at the culprit, I said "You are that man." He was immediately remorseful. He repented and was restored. If I had confronted him with accusations he would have become defensive. The story allowed him to see his sin for what it was.

Story is a powerful tool.

Checklist

- Do you love the young people in your community unconditionally?

- Are you willing to accept them even when you don't approve of their lifestyle?

- What life experiences can you draw from to build a bridge into their lives?

- Start a story file. When you read an interesting article or story you might be able to use, copy and paste it in your file. This will help if you are not good at creating your own illustrations.

- For those of you who are creative and up for the challenge; turn your experiences into short teachable story moments. People remember a story long after they've forgotten the facts.

- What needs are the young people in your community facing?

- What steps can you take to meet their needs?

14

P r i s o n e r s   o f   W a r

JESUS WAS KNOWN AS "a friend to sinners" (Luke 7:34), yet sometimes we the Church believe the lie that we need to avoid the bad kids. We have the mindset that these bad kids—sinners—are the enemy. We need to remember that we are all sinners—we were all enemies of God before He came to us and reconciled us to himself.

Peter had this, "us against them attitude", remember?

Acts 10 tells of an encounter between Cornelius, a Gentile, and an angel of God. The angel tells Cornelius to send for Peter. So Cornelius sent two servants to retrieve him.

About noon the following day as they were on their journey and approaching the city, Peter went up on the roof to pray. He became hungry and wanted something to eat, and while the meal was being prepared, he fell into a trance. He saw heaven opened and something like a large sheet being let down to earth by its four corners. It contained all kinds of four-footed animals, as well as reptiles and birds.

Then a voice told him, "Get up, Peter. Kill and eat."

"Surely not, Lord!" Peter replied. "I have never eaten anything impure or unclean."

The voice spoke to him a second time, "Do not call anything impure that God has made clean."

This happened three times, and immediately the sheet was taken back to heaven.

While Peter was wondering about the meaning of the vision, the men sent by Cornelius found out where Simon's house was and stopped at the gate. They called out, asking if Simon who was known as Peter was staying there.

While Peter was still thinking about the vision, the Spirit said to him, "Simon, three[a] men are looking for you. So get up and go downstairs. Do not hesitate to go with them, for I have sent them."

Peter went down and said to the men, "I'm the one you're looking for. Why have you come?"

The men replied, "We have come from Cornelius the centurion. He is a righteous and God-fearing man, who is respected by all the Jewish people. A holy angel told him to ask you to come to his house so that he could hear what you have to say." Then Peter invited the men into the house to be his guests.

The next day Peter started out with them, and some of the believers from Joppa went along. The following day he arrived in Caesarea. Cornelius was expecting them and had called together his relatives and close friends. As Peter entered the house, Cornelius met him and fell at his feet in reverence. But Peter made him get up. "Stand up," he said, "I am only a man myself."

While talking with him, Peter went inside and found a large gathering of people. He said to them: "You are well aware that it is against our law for a Jew to associate with or visit a Gentile. But God has shown me that I should not call anyone impure or unclean. So when I was sent for, I came without raising any objection. May I ask why you sent for me?"

—Acts 10:9-29

This happened three times, and immediately the sheet was taken back into heaven.

So Peter comes out of the trance and he's wondering what that was all about when the Gentile servants come looking for him. The Spirit tells him to go with them, so he does. Finally Peter gets it and in verse 28 he says, "You are well aware that it is against our law for a Jew to associate with a Gentile or visit him. But God has shown me that I should not call any man impure or unclean."

In the Gospel of Matthew Jesus is having dinner at Matthew's house. Matthew was a tax collector and despised by the religious community. Let's see how Jesus handled the situation.

> *While Jesus was having dinner at Matthew's house, many tax collectors and "sinners" came and ate with him and his disciples. When the Pharisees saw this, they asked the disciples, "Why does your teacher eat with tax collectors and "sinners?"*
>
> *On hearing this, Jesus said, "It is not the healthy who need a doctor, but the sick. But go and learn what this means: 'I desire mercy, not sacrifice.' For I have not come to call the righteous, but sinners."*
>
> —*Matthew 9:10-12*

We need to adopt this philosophy and remember that, while we were yet sinners, Christ died for us. We also need to remember that we are still sinners in need of forgiveness.

I have visited many churches where the adults did not want their kids to be around "sinners.". Paul asks a very important question in Romans 10:14: *How, then, can they call on the one they have not believed in? And how can they believe in the one of whom they have not heard? And how can they hear without someone preaching to them?*

Allow the kids in your youth ministry to let their light shine before men. Do not segregate them from a world that needs to hear the good news from them. It they are taught as kids to avoid unbelievers, they will grow into adults who don't share their faith with anyone.

Over the last decade we have been at war in the Middle East. I'm sure you've seen video on the nightly news of a shackled American soldier surrounded by al Qaeda in black masks. They have even posted gruesome videos of the beheading of our POWs on the news and Internet. Every time we hear a soldier has been captured, we fear for his life and unit in prayer, begging for his safe release.

We would never just throw our hands up and say "This generation of POWs is out of control" or "I hope these POWs get what they got coming to them." Would anyone dare say, "They should have known better?"

These statements would be ridiculous as well as heartless. We know these POWs were captured by the enemy and are in need of rescue. The enemy wants to destroy them and we want them to be saved.

We should treat every unbelieving teenager as a POW, captured by the enemy, united in prayer for their release from bondage. We should intervene and fight for their lives. But we don't.

All too often, after we observe these teens in sin we say, "I hope they get what they deserve. What is this generation coming too? Stay away from them— they are no good. Don't associate with them. They will only drag you down."

We are in a spiritual war against an enemy who has taken our young people captive, and we sit by in judgment and do nothing, allowing the enemy to win.

The sad thing is, adults are responsible for this generation's demise. *Project X* was a movie shown in theaters that was written and filmed by adults and marketed to teenagers. The movie is filled with teens drinking, having sex, and damaging property. The movie has spawned real life copycats that have resulted in hundreds of thousands of dollars in damage and several deaths.

WE SHOULD TREAT EVERY UNBELIEVING TEENAGER AS A POW, CAPTURED BY THE ENEMY.

Internet porn is made by adults, not teens, but the teens get addicted to it. Drugs are produced by adults and sold to young people. Cigarettes and alcohol are manufactured and distributed by adults. So when you see bad behavior and wonder what is wrong with this generation, the problem is us.

It's time to take back what the enemy is stealing from us—the lives and futures of our young people.

The only thing evil needs in order to succeed are Christians committed to doing nothing. Get off the pew and into the game.

15

A Working Model

I'VE LEARNED A LOT WORKING over two decades in youth outreach and ministry.

While it is true that when I started the ministry I didn't know how to marry this parachurch ministry and the traditional church, I've since learned we need each other.

Not everyone has the resources to rent a storefront and cover all the expenses involved with reaching these young people.

But every town has several or more churches with facilities to accommodate the needs of the youth in their town. Their churches are full of people who are more than capable of volunteering and mentoring these young people.

I knew, out of necessity, we had to find a way to bridge the gap between the two.

When you get a puppy, you can't just bring him into your home and let him have free roam. He will pee and poop all over the floor and chew everything in sight

You need to cordon him off. You put him in the mudroom and put up a baby gate. You work on potty training him. You train him not to chew on your stuff. After a time, you introduce him into the rest of the home.

Now he knows how to act. He's matured, so to speak. You feel confident leaving him alone in your home and know you will not come home to a mess. He may mess up every now and then, but for the most part, things are great.

Every day we meet teens that have never been to church. They have bad habits and don't understand that you shouldn't drop the F bomb during Friday night youth group. They may not think before they have sexually explicit conversations in front of your church kids.

Over the years though, I've found spending extensive time with these kids on the street and positive reinforcement goes a long way to solve these issues. These things result in a higher success rate when we do finally introduce them to the church. They see how we act, and find pride in themselves when they learn to act the same.

I've also helped churches prepare the church kids on what to expect and how to minister to these teens without judging them.

As I said before and reiterate now, fishing is messy and smelly. When you cast your lines into a broken, lost world, you will be dealing with people who have lots of problems.

We cannot expect people who do not have the Holy Spirit to live as if they do. When we grasp this truth, barriers are broken. If we expect the worst and ask God to give us His heart for them, we are on our way to building bridges, opening lines of communication, and possibly changing someone's eternity.

> WE CANNOT EXPECT PEOPLE WHO DO NOT HAVE THE HOLY SPIRIT TO LIVE AS IF THEY DO.

In August of 2014 I, along with my wife and son, traveled to Westerly Rhode Island to speak at a church. This church had heard about our success reaching young people and then ultimately whole families.

The pastor had arranged for area youth to meet at his church that Friday night for a youth rally. Then the following Saturday morning, I would teach the leaders in his church some of the things we were successfully doing to reach teens in our community.

My goal was to give them proven methods they could implement in their traditional church environment.

When I was greeted by a roomful of smiling faces, eager to learn how to make an impact in the lives of the young people in their community, I was encouraged.

The training session went extremely well. I returned to my hotel, looking forward to attending and speaking at the Sunday morning service the following day.

Word had spread about the training session the previous day, and Sunday morning I arrived to find more eager, smiling faces.

I gave a message titled *Zombie Church*. The pastor was a little concerned this Assemblies of God congregation would have trouble receiving this "Zombie" message. He could not have been more wrong. As part of my fundraising efforts whenever I speak, I sell *Zombie Church* T-shirts I've designed and printed. After the service, everyone present bought a shirt.

We went back to the pastor's house after the service and he discussed his personal disillusionment of his church with me. His church was only five years old and declining in numbers. At one point they had over a hundred people attending, but now they were hemorrhaging people and were down to under forty. He did not know how much longer they could hold on if things did not turn around.

After the training session on Saturday, I felt God speaking to me. I believed he was telling me to move to Rhode Island for a period of time to help this church. I hadn't mentioned this fact to my wife because I had promised her we would not move again, at least for a few years. But Sunday morning, after the service and before the pastor shared his concerns with me, my wife had come to me and told me she felt like

God was telling her we were supposed to move to Rhode Island to help the church. I could not help but smile.

She then told me she didn't want to tell our ten-year-old son this because she hated to move him away from all his friends and family.

Meantime, our son was upstairs playing Legos® with the pastor's son in his bedroom. He came down a few minutes later and said, "Hey guys, I think we should move here. I just feel like God is telling me we should move here."

Armed with the confirmed vision that we were supposed to help this church, I smiled as the pastor recounted his concerns.

After he was done speaking, I told him that we had heard from God and would be moving to Rhode Island to help him.

This was the perfect opportunity to modify and test my parachurch outreach methods and theories in a traditional church environment.

I was scheduled to deliver my final message at the Sunday evening service. When I arrived, every single person, and I mean everyone, including the pastor, was wearing a "*Zombie Church*" shirt. It was amazing. Under the "*Zombie Church*" inscription, the following verse is printed:

I know your deeds; you have a reputation for being alive, but you are dead. Wake up! Strengthen what remains and is about to die, for I have found your deeds unfinished in the sight of my God.

—Revelation 3:1-2

I announced to the congregation our plans to move to their community and help with outreach and creating disciples, who in turn would make more disciples.

Two months later we were living in Rhode Island. God moved and the church doubled in size within eight weeks.

We arrived on an afternoon in October. My son looked out the window and saw about ten young boys in the neighbor's yard playing kickball. He asked, "Hey dad, do you think I should go build some relationships with them?"

My son Christian, who was ten at the time, had only been six months old when we launched *252 Underground* in our home. He was raised up in ministry and outreach. He heard me speak to churches many times. He knows what it takes to reach young people.

I like to call him our Trojan Horse. He likes to go in and build friendships with kids then invite them back to our house, knowing that we will step up and do what we do best.

That's how we look at relational evangelism. We make the contact, build a friendship, and point kids to Jesus. Jesus then steps in and does what He does best.

My son Christian went over to where the kids were playing, introduced himself, and joined the game. I watched from my front porch. They started playing hide-and-seek. After a bit, I took one of seventy-five Nerf guns I had bought for "ministry" and headed over to where the kids were playing.

When they saw the Nerf gun, they all came running. I asked who wanted to have a massive Nerf gun war. Which was a stupid question. They all jumped up and down with excitement.

They followed my son and me across the street and freaked out when they saw all the brightly colored Nerf guns I had deliberately sprawled out in my living room with hundreds of rounds of ammunition (Nerf darts). They each grabbed a gun and handfuls of ammo. We ran back outside and had a killer Nerf gun war.

I told the kids that we were having another Nerf gun war and pizza party at the church on Sunday, (I made that up on the spot), and that they were invited. I told them to tell their parents they could come too.

I also invited them over the following night to eat dinner, play board games, and enjoy some snacks with some of my friends. (I made that up on the spot as well).

I went home and called some people from the church and told them to come over to my house the next night, just in case any of these kids showed up.

The next night at 6:00 p.m. a group of church people piled into my living room, but even better than that, the kids we had met the previous night came.

We ate tons of spaghetti and a bunch of junk food. The church folks bonded with the kids and everyone had a blast.

I invited the kids to come back Friday night for pretty much more of the same and reminded them about church Sunday and the pizza party/Nerf war.

Our first successful connection happened because a ten-year-old boy saw an opportunity to build relationships with neighborhood kids.

Expensive programs are not needed. No twelve week complicated training programs are necessary—just a love for the people around you. Taking time to get involved in their lives and inviting them to be a part of yours will bring them in.

Friday night our house was packed again. Some of the kids even brought friends. We ate more food, played Zombiopoly, Scrabble, and a bunch of other games. We asked the kids questions about their families, favorite sports teams, hobbies, school, etc.

The kids poured their hearts out to us. It was like no one had ever taken an interest in them. They shared about problems between their parents and problems in school. Nothing was off limits.

We had known these kids less than a week, and I now knew more about some of them than people I had known for years. The church people were shocked at how easy this was.

They had bought into the myth that evangelism is something you do, not something you live. We were living out our faith in this community. The kids got wind of something and came to get a taste.

What they didn't know at the time was they were getting a taste of Jesus. It was Friday night, but Sunday was coming.

Discussion Points

- What is your "Nerf gun"?
- What would it take to have a weekly game night at your house?
- Would your church be willing to host a "Pizza Party" for the young people in your neighborhood?
- What would it look like to put together an outreach team of neighborhood missionaries?
- Could you start a neighborhood or church dodgeball league?
- What are the kids in your community interested in?

16

Shooting Our Way Into Their Hearts

I WOKE UP EARLY SUNDAY MORNING excited about the possibilities the impact of a simple Nerf gun war and pizza could have on this community of young people.

Before we moved to Westerly, Rhode Island, many well-meaning friends told us not to waste our time. New England was spiritually dead and one of the hardest places to grow a church. We were told statistics prove New Englanders are resistant to the Word of God.

On my first visit to Rhode Island, prior to making the commitment to move there, I visited a few churches and spoke to the pastors. They told me the same things.

They shared how they struggled to maintain the few people they had. They thought "growth" was a foreign concept. Their youth groups consisted of fewer than ten kids.

I politely listened to their plight but I imagined the Israelites shaking in their armor as they faced the Philistines led by a giant of a man named Goliath.

They were scared. They gave many reasons why they could not defeat the army. By the world's standard, they were probably right. The army was more powerful than they were. But what they failed to understand was the simple truth that the army was not more powerful than God.

Then along comes this shepherd boy. He sees the same sight they do. But he chooses to see the situation through the lens of faith.

> *David said to Saul, "Let no one lose heart on account of this Philistine; your servant will go and fight him."*
>
> *Saul replied, "You are not able to go out against this Philistine and fight him; you are only a young man and he has been a warrior from his youth."*
>
> *—1 Samuel 17:32*

Saul was focused on the negative. By the world's standard, he was right to be concerned. But Saul had forgotten the one thing he had going for him.

David was undeterred and focused on one important fact.

> *David said to the Philistine, "You come against me with sword and spear and javelin, but I come against you in the name of the LORD Almighty, the God of the armies of Israel, whom you have defied."*
>
> *—1 Samuel 17:45*

The people who told me it could not be done, that we could not grow a church in Westerly Rhode Island, had lost sight of the power in the One whom they served.

They had allowed the enemy to intimidate them. They were shaking in their armor. Mentally defeated, they had given up. The enemy had stolen the territory that belonged to God and they were resigned to the "fact" they could not win.

THEY HAD ALLOWED THE ENEMY TO INTIMIDATE THEM.

Yes, it's true. We cannot do anything in our own power *BUT*, greater is He that is in us than he that is in the world!

> *You, dear children, are from God and have overcome them, because the one who is in you is greater than the one who is in the world. They are from the world and speak from the viewpoint of the world, and therefore the world listens to*

them. We are from God, and whoever knows God, listens to us; but whoever is not from God does not listen to us. This is how we recognize the Spirit of truth and the spirit of falsehood.

—1 John 4:4-6

If I can guarantee one thing, it is this: when you set out to fight the enemy and win souls for Christ, you are entering a realm that you are not welcome in. You are taking back territory the enemy has claimed for himself. You will be attacked.

Satan will use your closest friends to discourage you. They will give you a thousand reasons why your God-given vision cannot be done. You will find yourself surrounded by negativity. Keep pressing in. When you feel alone in the battle, keep pressing in. When the giants stand in front of you and defy your God, do not turn and run.

Stand and fight. It does not matter what stands in your way. It does not matter how many come against you. They cannot stop the One who is in you.

The enemy will try to get you to doubt your calling and disqualify yourself. Satan will point out all your weaknesses. He will throw whatever he can at you to trip you up.

When you find yourself in these valleys of self-doubt, remember this promise from Jesus:

Very truly I tell you, whoever believes in me will do even greater things than these, because I am going to the Father.

—John 14:12

How is this possible? Are we greater than Jesus? The reason we will do greater things is not because we have greater abilities than Jesus but because we've been given the gift of the Holy Spirit. He uses us to accomplish great things. Impossible things.

When people told me all the reasons why we could not reach people in Westerly, Rhode Island, I knew what they were saying was the absolute truth. I could not reach anyone ... on my own. However, I was just a small part of the equation.

Thankfully, I did not plan on reaching anyone on my own. I spent time in prayer. I had ministry partners praying for the mission. Unlike the time I got ahead of God when launching *252 Underground*, this time I waited on the Lord.

I knew that the Holy Spirit was going ahead of us into Westerly, Rhode Island to plow the hard gravel dirt of people's hearts. I trusted Him to prepare the soil for the seed He was sending me and my family to plant.

So that Sunday morning when I awoke, I was not anxious. I knew God would send whoever He planned on sending. Worrying about whether anyone would show was just a waste of time.

My son and I loaded up the back of my pickup truck with the seventy-five Nerf guns, snacks, and sodas. We arrived at the church early and within minutes the kids arrived.

I greeted then corralled the excited kids, passed out snacks and drinks, and shared a Bible story with them.

After church I ordered pizzas, and we had a two hour Nerf gun war in the parking lot. We ate pizza, drank sodas and built friendships and trust. That was the first of many Sundays spent like this.

Most every day the kids brought friends to my house. We fed them, mostly spaghetti, played board and video games, and shot each other with hundreds of Nerf bullets.

Over the course of a few weeks, our house became a haven for these young people searching for meaning. They shared their life stories with us. Their dysfunctional home lives broke our hearts. But they felt a peace at our house. Many admitted they wished our house was their home.

OUR HOUSE BECAME A HAVEN FOR THESE YOUNG PEOPLE SEARCHING FOR MEANING.

When we arrived at the church in Westerly, there were only four kids in the church, all under six years of age. Things changed quickly when we started a Wednesday program to teach Bible stories to these young people who had no Bible knowledge.

In three weeks they had memorized all sixty-six books in the Bible. They were hungry for God's Word and ate every word we fed them.

And within weeks, it happened. Parents started coming to our house with their kids. We ate meals together and played games almost every night. I don't think we had one day in seven months that someone was not in our home.

We built relationships with these parents. They saw something in us they didn't have. They said they felt good when they were with us and felt better about themselves.

What they were experiencing was the love of Jesus, for them, through us. Some even started attending church. In seven weeks the church's Sunday morning attendance grew from thirty-nine adults to sixty-nine.

The children's ministry had about thirty on any given week. Older siblings started coming to our house so we opened up our home Friday nights for a *252 Underground* outreach. The teens came and we loved on them and fed them. They shared with us what was on their minds and hearts. We talked about school, their home life, and their future. These Friday nights at our house became the highlight of their week.

My wife and I laughed about that; we were not doing anything really special. We simply gave them the love and attention they lacked. We played board games and ate spaghetti, but to these kids it was special.

We knew that we could not just focus on the kids if we wanted to see real change in the community. We needed to help the parents if we were going to make a lasting impact in the homes of these young people.

I started a weekly Bible study with two groups of men, and my wife met with two women. The men and I met at the *Dunkin' Donuts*. Two men and I met on Tuesday night, and another two men and I met on Thursday night.

We read tons of Scripture and talked about issues affecting their lives. I taught the men what the Bible said about being a loving husband and what a godly father looked like. We saw lives change and it was easy, because the Holy Spirit was doing what He does best.

We did many things to bring these families together. We took groups to the movies, the beach, skateboard parks, and community picnics.

Simple things done in the love of Jesus provided extraordinary results. Our time in Rhode Island proved fruitful. I have many fond memories of our time there and I know we made an eternal impact.

If we would have listened to the people who told us it was not possible, we would have missed out on a ton of blessing.

If you know God wants you to step out in faith, His voice is the only voice you need to listen to.

Discussion Points

- What giants are keeping you from accomplishing God's call on your life?
- Do you have a support team to encourage and pray for you when you face the doubters?
- What are some things you could start doing now to make an impact in your community?
- If you started a small Bible study group, who would you invite? Think about people without any Bible knowledge.

17

The Perfect Marriage

IN SEPTEMBER 2015 I WAS OFFERED the job of Senior
Pastor at a church in Northeast Philadelphia. We had been praying
about the direction God wanted us to go after our one year commitment
in Rhode Island came to an end.

I had never been a senior pastor before. I had never been to
seminary or attended college for that matter.

My wife always believed I was too "outside the box" to be a pastor
in a traditional church. I dance to the beat of a different drum. While
this may have been true, we both felt God was opening doors with this
opportunity.

We prayed, put out our "fleeces," and God answered. We would move back to Pennsylvania, where I would pastor a Lutheran church though I was not even a Lutheran.

I officially took over the helm in November 2015 when the previous pastor left.

Overwhelmed, scared, and under qualified, God would yet reveal His strength through my weaknesses.

The congregation was an older one, with many people over sixty. Self-contained for so long, they had failed to reach out to their community and were most likely ten years from having to close the church doors. Married to the "glory days" when the church was 650 strong, it was now on life support with 70 folks attending Sunday morning services.

THEY HAD FAILED TO REACH OUT TO THEIR COMMUNITY.

Ninety years old, the church looked like a Gothic castle with a 1950s addition and had fallen into disrepair. When I first laid eyes on it, I envisioned transforming it into a community center with a coffee bar/concession stand and a movie theater where families could come out and watch positive movies. I pictured youth hanging out on a Friday night, eating hot meals, playing video games, Ping Pong, basketball, dodgeball, and hearing the truths of God's Word.

I saw coffeehouse get-togethers with live music and strangers becoming friends. I envisioned game nights where people from the community could gather together around tables playing Monopoly, Jenga, chess, and Life.

It took almost four months to bring the old building back to life. On March 4th, 2016 we opened our first coffeehouse. It was attended by 125 people. We even gave away a 42 inch flat screen TV.

All the things I had envisioned have come to pass. Attendance has tripled.

Since launching *252 Underground*, young people from the surrounding community now attend. We do many of the same things we did when we rented a storefront, and we've had the privilege of leading many to Christ.

The young people now come to church—on their own—without their parents. They are hungry for God. We love them. We meet their needs. And I teach them in creative and practical ways. Parents are beginning to wander in with their kids Sunday mornings.

In the beginning, I honestly didn't know if I could build this ministry in a traditional church, but I learned if I spend time out in the community building relationships, I have a higher success rate within the walls of the church. My mantra is: *Stop bringing people to Jesus, instead, let's take Jesus to the people.* And it works.

When I worked in a church twenty years ago, I would go out, see a kid, and just invite him to church. These young people who I had no relationship with dismissed me as just another Jesus freak or Holy Roller.

Then I learned the value of building relationship bridges that give me the right to speak into their lives. As I've spent time developing trust and respect outside the walls of the church, it feels natural when I invite them to our coffeehouse or game night at the church. I'm their friend Rob, not some religious zealot or nut ball.

These young people look forward to getting together. Relational evangelism is the key to reaching young people in a traditional church setting.

Get out in your community. Prayer-walk the neighborhoods around your church. Ask the Holy Spirit to soften and prepare the hearts of the people inside these homes.

Go to the local parks. Pass out drinks and snacks with no strings attached.

Have a "Movie-under-the-Stars" night. Put a blowup movie screen (Target.com $135.00) on your church lawn or in your parking lot. Pick a movie that does not ram the gospel down their throats. Get some candy, popcorn, and sodas. Mail postcards or have some volunteers pass out some door hangers in the neighborhoods you have prayer-walked.

Or get a permit to close down a street by your church. Rent a moon bounce and dunk tank. Build some carnival type games like corn hole. Buy some prizes from the party store. Set up some canopies and give out hotdogs and chips. Have your church band or youth band play. Get active in the community.

This past October we built a small stage and set it up on the grass next to my church. We purchased bales of hay and cornstalks, and built a big fire pit. On a Sunday night we played acoustic music, ate hot dogs, cookies, and made a ton of s'mores. We called it "Fireside Church" and invited the community. They came in droves. We even set up a 10 x 20 canopy with pumpkins and markers for the kids to decorate their own pumpkin. It was a huge success.

If your church were to close its doors, would the community care or even notice? If our doors ever close, the community will feel the loss because we've become a part of it.

We need to stop hiding behind our stained glass windows and take Jesus out into a lost and hurting world. That's the only way the church will have a lasting impact.

Discussion Points

- What are you willing to do to reach your community with the message of the Gospel?
- What are you willing to spend?
- What are some tangible things you could do to build bridges with the people in your churches' neighborhood?
- Could you put a team together to brainstorm some ideas to reach the young people in your community?
- What would it look like if you took Jesus outside the walls of your church?

18

C H I L   O u t

252 UNDERGROUND BIRTHED another awesome ministry geared towards college-aged teens. It grew out of necessity as well as demand.

At *252 Underground* we have policies in place to protect our young people. One of those entails keeping older teens who have graduated high school from hanging out with the younger teens. We did not want eighteen year old guys trying to hook up with fifteen year old girls, and neither do you.

Although I believe in this policy, I hated the fact that after we mentored and grown to love these kids, we had to throw them back out in the world at the very age we lose them in churches.

We had to do something to stay connected with them, but I was not sure what that was and what it would look like. College-age kids are searching for meaning and a place to fit in, and we wanted to provide that for them at this crucial stage in their life. With twenty-five bars in a 1.6 square mile area of our youth ministry, I prayed for a solution that would provide them healthy alternatives and felt God leading me to add a college ministry.

Since we were not using our building on Saturday nights, we launched CHIL, an acronym for Christ Happening In Lives, on Saturday nights from 7:00 p.m. to 11:00 p.m. It was an instant success. We followed the same format, and did not announce the fact we were faith-based. We just loved them where they were and saw explosive growth, from twenty people that first night totwo-hundred in five months. What started out as a program for our graduated teens quickly attracted people who had never attended our *252 Underground* program.

Even though we used the same building, Saturday nights had a totally different vibe with an added coffee bar and more substantial meals for a donation, if they had it. An Internet café and Cable TV for sporting events helped us develop a lot of great relationships, and we were able to share the gospel with them through open communication and a short relevant message. Some asked for the chance to give a message and we let them. They did a great job and it encouraged others to give it a shot. Some *252 Underground* leaders were born out of CHIL.

Christ Happening in Lives (CHIL)

This ministry can easily be duplicated. If you have a gymnasium or some extra space that could be turned into a coffeehouse on Saturday nights, you would be filling a void in the lives of many young people.

As they head off to college, young people tend to sever ties with the church they grew up in. They feel like they don't fit in. Too old to attend youth group, with no connection to the church, many fall away.

TOO OLD TO ATTEND YOUTH GROUP, WITH NO CONNECTION TO THE CHURCH, MANY FALL AWAY.

CHIL offers the opportunity to reconnect with these college-age kids in a relevant, exciting way, and provides a healthy alternative to the street. Some of these same young people helped us reach out to the victims of that fire I mentioned earlier. When filled with passion and purpose, young people can turn the world upside down for Christ. Look at the life of Timothy.

Timothy was just a young man, some say maybe even as young as seventeen. Paul mentored him and poured into him, just as Jesus did with the disciples. Like most young people, Timothy absorbed things like a sponge. Young people are not as jaded as some of us older folks can be. They are more optimistic and still believe all things are possible.

When we let these young people, filled with the Holy Spirit, loose on a community, stand back and watch things happen. Many of these same young people have facilitated positive change in the lives of their campus friends who have never met us or stepped foot in our building.

In making a positive impact one young person at a time, we are teaching and equipping them to be disciples who make disciples. They then find local churches to attend and even become involved in ministries there. I've performed weddings for these same young people, and have written reference letters to help them in career positions.

It has been amazing to watch what we planted ten or more years ago grow and flourish and produce a crop—thirty, sixty, and a hundred-fold.

19

Develop Leaders

IN THE EARLY YEARS OF OUR MINISTRY, I spent countless hours pouring my heart and soul into the lives of young people, only to see my efforts choked out by the *natural* leader of the group. You know the one I'm talking about. The kid that everyone looks up to and tries to emulate.

Time and again this left me frustrated. So much time and energy spent, only to have all my progress undone by the influence of one kid.

Then I had an epiphany. Why not go straight to the top? I looked for the one the others looked up to and proceeded to invest in that kid's development.

Seek out the natural leader and pour yourself into his/her life. When he is changed, he will lead the revolution.

Jesus led in this area by example. Although Jesus did not choose the popular people, He did choose a core group to mentor. He spoke to large crowds numbering in the thousands, had an entourage of about a hundred, but poured everything into twelve men. .

He shared His life with them, and taught them with actions more than words. He endured hardships and persecution with them, and over the course of a few years, Jesus' mission became theirs. By meeting their needs and loving them, He earned the right to be heard. He was a teacher but more than that, He was their friend.

BY MEETING THEIR NEEDS AND LOVING THEM, HE EARNED THE RIGHT TO BE HEARD.

Jesus took twelve ordinary men and turned them into professional evangelists, world-class fishers of men. It is because of these men that you and I even know the name of Jesus. If it were not for them, there would be no church today.

In your community, I guarantee you will find young people that you can pour into. Men and women who will grow into world-class fishers of men. But remember it's not a quick hit-and-run—it's a time consuming process and you will face setbacks. Even Jesus experienced setbacks with the disciples.

Check out an instance from Mark:

"What are you arguing with them about?" Jesus asked. A man in the crowd answered, "Teacher, I brought you my son, who is possessed by a spirit that has robbed him of speech.

Whenever it seizes him, it throws him to the ground. He foams at the mouth, gnashes his teeth and becomes rigid. I asked your disciples to drive out the spirit but they could not."

"You unbelieving generation," Jesus replied, "how long shall I stay with you? How long shall I put up with you? Bring me the boy."

—Mark 9:16-19

20

Don't Quit

I'VE SHARED WITH YOU a lot of awesome things that God has accomplished through the ministries of *252 Underground*, but we've had more than our fair share of disappointments.

As I've said before, I often wondered if we were making a lasting impact. Although we saw changes in the lives of many young people, there were many others who did not change.

We continuously poured into them without any visible results. They continued to drink, smoke and take drugs. They boasted about the sex they were having and posted all kinds of profanity on their Facebook pages.

I began to doubt the whole program and started to feel I was wasting time in fruitless endeavors, especially when I thought about the sacrifices my family and I had made.

If you have been involved in youth ministry for any length of time you have probably had similar feelings at some point.

We want to see positive results with accompanying actions. We want to see young people deep in prayer and carrying their Bibles around. We want to see the young women dress modestly and the guys act like gentlemen.

We want them evangelizing their friends and bringing them to youth group. These things are the mark of a successful youth ministry, right? It's why we pour countless hours of our life into these kids. The reason we go on all those youth trips instead of family vacations. The motivation for spending every Friday night with a group of "wild animals" for four hours instead of dinner and a movie with our spouse or own family.

We want to see transformed lives that in turn transform more lives. That is why I thought I was doing it. While these are noble reasons, upon reflection I've decided they are unrealistic expectations planted by the enemy.

We are laying foundations and planting oak trees. You can't judge whether you are successful by what you see in front of you today or next month. You need to look ten years or more down the road.

I cannot guarantee what you will get from your investment, but if you don't invest in the lives of these young people, I promise you'll get nothing.

As I battled with doubt, God revealed a Scripture to me. He is good like that.

What, after all, is Apollos? And what is Paul? Only servants, through whom you came to believe—as the Lord has assigned to each his task. I planted the seed and Apollos watered it but God made it grow. So neither he who plants nor he who waters is anything, but only God, who makes things grow. The man who plants and the man who waters have one purpose, and each will be rewarded according to his own labor. For we are God's fellow workers; you are God's field, God's building.

—1 Corinthians 3:6-9

I was trying to do God's job and beating myself up when I failed. Reading this Scripture, the pressure fell away. I realized I am doing exactly what God has called me to and requires of me. He will reward my efforts.

Always remember, we are in this for the long haul. Planting, fertilizing, watering, and harvesting. The growth is up to God, in His timing. Let's not try to do God's job. We are grossly under qualified.

The Old Testament prophets called for revival and many times revival did not happen. We are not responsible for the revival or the growth but only the effort.

Jesus shared this truth in the Parable of the Growing Seed:

> *This is what the kingdom of God is like. A man scatters seed on the ground. Night and day, whether he sleeps or gets up, the seed sprouts and grows, though he does not know how.*
>
> *All by itself the soil produces grain- first the stalk, then the head, then the full kernel in the head. As soon as the grain is ripe, he puts the sickle to it, because the harvest has come.*
>
> —Mark 4:26-29

IF YOU THROW IN THE TOWEL, SATAN WINS.

Don't set yourself up for failure; leave the growth to God. Don't get discouraged when you don't see spectacular results. If you do become discouraged, don't quit. Remember this is the enemy's plan to stop the advancement of God's Kingdom.

If you throw in the towel, Satan wins. Remember the only way evil prevails is when good men do nothing.

TO BE CONTINUED...

APPENDIX

Sample Lessons

I WANTED TO SHARE WITH YOU some blogs I wrote that you can use as quick teaching moments with the young people you connect with.

Lesson 1:
You Hungry?

So check out the story in John 6:1-13 where Jesus fed five-thousand hungry dudes plus all their wives and rug rats. I can't even begin to comprehend something so insane, but I want to focus on a part of the story that often gets overlooked.

Yes, it's totally amazing that Jesus took five loaves and two fish and multiplied them into a feast that fed fifteen thousand when you include the women and children. I don't want to take away from that, but let's look at a seemingly insignificant character in the story.

Why do I say they are insignificant, and who am I talking about? I'm glad you asked these important questions. Let me enlighten you.

First, the person I'm speaking of is the boy with the fish sandwiches. And to answer your question about his insignificance, the Gospel of John is the only book that even records his actions. This same story is told in Matthew, Mark, and Luke, yet they don't mention the boy.

Why not? It seems the authors of these other books were focused on the miracle itself, and not what made the miracle possible. But I think this young boy's actions warrants some discussion and can, at the very least, serve to open our eyes to what is possible when we give God what we have.

Be Prepared

Out of fifteen thousand people, the boy was the only one prepared. Five loaves of bread and two fish would be quite a lunch for a small boy. It might even provide him dinner should this teacher talk on into the night.

Give What You Have

So here he is, a young boy clutching his sack lunch, surrounded by fifteen thousand unprepared, hungry people. How many of us would think, "Too bad, you should have planned ahead," "It's not my problem," or "I only have enough for myself."?

If the boy had these thoughts, he did not act on them. He took the little he had and gave it to the disciples who in turn gave it to Jesus. If you think about the scene for a minute, you will understand the significance of his actions.

Picture This

You're out in a field far from any town, with fifteen thousand people. You're just a small boy and cannot even see Jesus. Your field of vision is a sea of butts. Some men are working their way through the crowd, and you hear that the Teacher needs food. Your stomach has been rumbling, and you were just thinking about the nice meal your bread and fish will make.

Yet, something makes you give it to the men instead. They immediately whisk you through the crowd, pushing people aside. Finally you are standing before the Teacher—so close you can touch Him. (Sacrificial giving always gets you closer to Jesus). They take your lunch and give it to Him. Goodbye lunch.

You have no way of knowing if it will make its way back to you. But you just knew this Teacher, the one you heard amazing stories about, needed your lunch. The boy willingly surrendered all he had to Jesus, expecting nothing in return.

Jesus did the miracle, but without the boy and his willingness to give what he had, things would have gone differently. I'm not saying Jesus could not have turned rocks into bread, but what I do know is God always works through a surrendered life.

Trust Jesus

Jesus can do more with a crumb than we can with a whole bread factory.

We need to trust that Jesus will take care of us when we put our lives in His hands, whatever that looks like. Jesus' will is better than our will. His plans are better and bigger than our plans. The boy John introduced us to ran his race to win an eternal prize.

JESUS' PLANS ARE BETTER AND BIGGER THAN OUR PLANS.

Here is a boy with five small barley loaves and two small fish, but how far will they go among so many?...

Don't let anyone tell you that you are too young or insignificant to make a difference in the Kingdom of God. Always remember, we are the hands and feet of Jesus.

Lesson 2:
Keep Planting

So I was reading the Parable of the Sower for like the umpteenth time and something struck me that I never paid attention to before.

This is going to sound stupid but I never claimed to be a rocket scientist. So what did I overlook a million times in the Parable of the Sower? The sower—the farmer planting the seeds.

Crazy I know, right? How could I overlook the sower? I mean, he's right there in the title. Nevertheless, I did. I was always focused on the soils receiving the seeds. I thought that was the crux of the parable and maybe it is, but humor me for the next minute or two.

Without the sower dude, there are no seeds being sown. And without seeds connecting with the soil, it won't matter how good the soil is, or how much sun or rain the soil receives—ain't nothing going to happen.

So the sower/farmer dude is the most important element in the cycle of growth. And in the parable, who do you think the farmer guy casting seeds represents? Yeah you got it. You and me.

My mind started doing that thing it does when a spark of insanity—oops I mean inspiration—strikes, and it starts kicking around up there in the grey matter. After the dust cleared out, I got some clarity.

If I owned a farm and had lots of acreage and tons of fancy machinery for planting crops and harvesting them, but I never planted a single solitary seed, ever, would you or anyone consider me a farmer?

Or what if I only planted one seed on my thousand acre farm? I would be a fool to expect a big harvest. You get what I'm saying?

I noticed three key points about the sower in the parable.

- He kept casting seeds even when things did not go the way he hoped. Birds ate them. Some did not take, and others started but died. But he was not deterred. He knew if he just kept casting seeds, eventually he would harvest a crop.
- He cast seeds everywhere. Along the path. In the rocks. Even in the thorny places. He didn't want to miss any place that might produce growth—he didn't prejudge the soil.
- His perseverance paid off. He enjoyed a huge crop many times over.

So what's our take-away from this?

When you plant the seeds of the gospel in someone's life, sometimes their friends or family will destroy the work you've done. They will talk them out of following Jesus. They will tell you are crazy or part of a cult.

KEEP PLANTING

Sometimes your friends might receive what you are saying. They with say a prayer and be excited, only to go to school and be ridiculed by their peers. They will turn back to their old ways to avoid persecution.

KEEP PLANTING

Sometimes your friends will listen, get excited, and maybe even come to church a few times. But then social media, attractions to the opposite sex, sports or work, and the pursuit of the next iPhone, will drown out their zeal for God.

KEEP PLANTING

YOU WILL EVENTUALLY FIND GOOD SOIL IN THE HEARTS OF YOUR FRIENDS.

If you diligently keep planting, you will eventually find good soil in the hearts of your friends. Something miraculous will occur and they will become sowers themselves. Together you will bring in a harvest.

KEEP PLANTING

Then he [Jesus] said to his disciples, "The harvest is plentiful but the workers are few. Ask the Lord of the harvest, therefore, to send out workers into his harvest field."

—Matthew 9:37-38 NIV

L e s s o n   3 :
S a l v a t i o n ' s   F r u i t

In the book of Luke, written by a guy named Luke, we read the story of Zacchaeus the tax collector. It's a fairly short story so I'm going to share it here with you and then we will dissect a few key truths we can take away from it.

Jesus entered Jericho and was just passing through. A man was there by the name of Zacchaeus. He was a chief tax collector, (a nice way to say; "dirty, rotten, scoundrel"), and he was wealthy. (Mainly because he was a "dirty, rotten, scoundrel").

He wanted to see who Jesus was, but because he was short (for the politically correct this means vertically challenged), and he could not see over the crowd.

So he ran ahead and climbed a sycamore tree to see Jesus since He was coming that way. When Jesus reached the spot, He looked up and said to him. "Zacchaeus come down immediately. I must stay at your house today."

So Zacchaeus came down at once and welcomed him gladly. All the people saw this and began to mutter, "He has gone to be the guest of a sinner."

But Zacchaeus stood and said to the Lord, "Look, Lord! Here and now I give half of my possessions to the poor, and if I have cheated anybody out of anything, (it was not a question of if, but just how many), I will pay back four times the amount."

Jesus said to him, "*Today salvation has come to this house, because this man, too, is a son of Abraham. For the Son of Man came to seek and save the lost.*" (Luke 19:9-10).

So what is our takeaway here? Let's unpack this story for a minute. For starters, did you see how Zacchaeus wanted to see who Jesus was?

He was curious. He had no doubt heard stories about this Jesus dude, and he wanted to check Him out to see if there was any truth to the rumors. But it goes a little deeper than that.

I think the Holy Spirit was doing a little heart surgery on Zacchaeus. The Bible says in Romans:

There is no one who understands; there is no one who seeks God.   —*Romans 3:11*

John backs it up:

No one can come to me, (Jesus), unless the Father who sent me draws them, I will raise them up at the last day.
—*John 6:44*

I always ask God to stir someone's heart before I speak to them about God, because half the battle is won right there. The Holy Spirit prepares the soil of their heart before I ever plant the seed.

I believe that's exactly what took place with Zacchaeus. The Holy Spirit stirred something in him and prodded him to want to know who this Jesus was.

If God is laying someone on your heart He wants you to share your faith with, you can be sure the Holy Spirit has been working and preparing them for you.

We can also see from this story, when someone is open to the gospel message, Jesus is not far away. Jesus met Zacchaeus right where he was at.

That's how Jesus operates—He comes to you. He meets you in the mess that is your life. Some religious-minded people want you to believe you need to clean up your act first, to get things right before coming to Jesus. That's like waiting to go to the hospital until the bleeding stops.

That's a lie from the enemy. If you remember the story of the prodigal son in Luke 15:11-32, the son realized he had messed up and wanted to return to his father. Verse 20 is key here:

> *While he was still a long way off, his father saw him and was filled with compassion for him; he ran to his son, threw his arms around him and kissed him.*

Satan wants you to feel guilt and shame. Your Father, God, just wants you back in His arms where you belong,

When Jesus confronted Zacchaeus and told him to come down, Zacchaeus responded immediately. When you have sinned and feel like you are separated from God, Satan will try to drive the wedge deeper.

Don't give the devil a foothold. Turn back to God immediately and repent.

Don't Prejudge

When Jesus called Zacchaeus, the religious leaders threw a hissy fit. They did not feel Zacchaeus was worthy. If they had their way, they would see Zacchaeus thrown into hell.

I can settle the debate right now. None of us deserves Jesus, but that's what grace and mercy are all about.

Here's the Real Kicker

Jesus did not require Zacchaeus to say the "Sinner's Prayer" to receive salvation. Zacchaeus' salvation came through a changed life when Zacchaeus stood up and said, "Lord, whatever I've done wrong, I will make right."

THAT'S IT!

YOUTHANIZE: THE DEATH OF TRADITIONAL YOUTH MINISTRY

There are many people who are told to just say this prayer and you are good. They recite a prayer and walk away unchanged. They produce no fruit. There is no evidence they've met Jesus.

They don't look different, act different, or talk different. They are completely unchanged by their "encounter" with Jesus.

The problem with this is they think they are "saved," but they are not. Repentance is turning from sin. Repentance is a change in direction. Yesterday I was going that way. Today I'm going this way with Jesus.

Satan uses the "Sinner's Prayer" to snare many people. He sells you the lie—just say this prayer, brother. That's all you need to do and you are good.

SATAN USES THE "SINNER'S PRAYER" TO SNARE MANY PEOPLE.

The scary thing is we Christians are his best salespeople. A changed life is the only evidence of salvation. If Jesus hasn't changed you, He hasn't saved you.

The devil wants you to just say a prayer. Jesus just wants you to let Him change your life.

Don't buy the lie

If there ain't no fruit

You've been duped!

Lesson 4: Counting on You

I'll start by telling you what I tell every young person I speak to: you are not the church of the future. You are the church of today. I don't care if you are only fifteen. Your age doesn't matter.

You are a necessary part of a properly functioning body of Christ. So I will treat you as such.

The church has lost its way over the years in many ways. She's forgotten her first love. The fire has gone out. Passion has left the building.

You have the privilege and duty to steer the ship back on course. It's up to you. It's hard for older folks set in their ways, to change.

But you ... everything changes around you in milliseconds. Plus you are passionate about everything you set your heart on. You are exactly what the church needs to ignite a fire in her belly.

So I'm going to put some stuff, heavy stuff, out there to give you a feel for how things are and how they should be. I'm going to give you a plan to lead you back to the church Jesus called us to be. We will look over the map together and see how to rebuild on a solid foundation.

We may have to take a wrecking ball to a few things, but you've got this—I've seen you in a mosh pit.

Excerpt:

Regener8

This is an excerpt from my teen devotional, REGENER8.

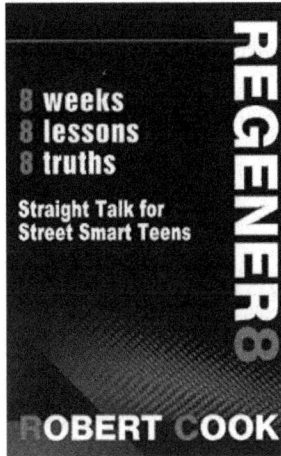

The Devil Made Me Do It

When we get busted for doing bad stuff, we blame everyone else. We don't want to take responsibility for our actions.

Grown men on trial for killing 127 people blame their parents and their childhood for their crimes. It's ridiculous but lawyers try anyway. It rarely works.

Here's Why

James, the brother of Jesus, sums it up best:

*"But each one is tempted, when, by **his own** evil desire, he is dragged away and enticed."*

—James 1:14, emphasis mine

Slippery Slope

James goes on to explain what happens when we smoke that first cigarette, drink that first beer, or smoke that first joint. It never stops there.

"Then after desire has conceived, it gives birth to sin, and sin, when it is full-grown, gives birth to death."

—James 1:15

Remember, the devil can't make you do anything you don't want to do. He can only make suggestions. You make the choices.

You Need A Shield

A shield can protect you from flaming arrows or, if you're Captain America, it can stop bullets. But you will probably never find yourself dodging bullets or flaming arrows.

There is a shield, though, that you can acquire to protect yourself against temptations that are guaranteed to come at you. It's called knowledge of the Bible.

"I have hidden your word in my heart that I might not sin against you"

—Psalm 119:11

What Good Is A Gun With No Bullets?

Having a Bible in your house and not ready it is like having a gun with no ammo. Either one is useless.

Take Fifteen

Minutes that is, and read the Book of James. It's short, but packed with great insight.

If you study the Word of God

You can use it to defeat Satan

Excerpt:

Illumin8

This is a sample devotional from my book, ILLUMIN8.

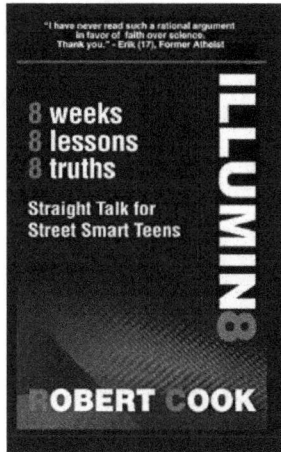

Do You Suffer from Narcotizing Dysfunction?

I recently joined a gym...again. Hopefully this time I'll actually go. I always convince myself I will use my gym membership since I'm paying good money for it. But somehow that does not relate to action.

In the months leading up to my joining the gym, I read several articles in *Men's Health* about the importance of exercise and proper diet. I researched and became well informed about the carious workouts featured in *Muscle & Fitness* magazine. I wanted a certain result. I purchased all the vitamins they recommended. I'm good to go.

I even tell my wife, "This time it's on. I'm doing it, baby." She rolls her eyes and laughs. I'm always surprised at her response. What does she know? I'll show her. Wait until I come home looking like Dwayne "The Rock" Johnson. Roll your eyes then, woman!

Fast Forward

Six months goes by quickly. I haven't seen my gym membership card in four months. It might be under the Whopper wrappers discarded on my nightstand. Or it could have gone through the wash. Who knows?

I look at all the unopened bottles of vitamins on my dresser and wonder if I can return them. My wife is not going to meet Dwayne "The Rock" Johnson. She'll have to settle for Robert "The Gut" Cook, but she already knew that.

What's Wrong with Me?

I did a Goggle search and found a disease with all my symptoms. *Narcotizing Dysfunction*. Was I going to die? Would it be painful? How long did I have?

I read on and was relieved to find it was not fatal. Narcotizing Dysfunction, a sociological condition that I've nicknamed "ND00." Those who suffer from it confuse knowledge with action. The idea is, the more they become informed, the less active they become.

They mistake knowing about something and even talking about it as doing something.

They can rationalize not doing anything because they have talked about it and are informed about it.

Wow, that's crazy, but awesome. At least now I could tell my wife I had a legitimate disease. I was sick.

Serious Condition

While my gym experience is somewhat humorous, when it comes to our spiritual lives, it's no laughing matter.

I experienced some of these symptoms in my faith journey. And I am not alone.

Many followers of Christ have a roller coaster relationship with Jesus. They are on fire in January when they are making New Year's Eve resolutions, but then in February, a cold front rolls in. The fire dwindles to a few embers. By March, the fire burns out.

The Vaccine

Unlike the infected Zombies in The Walking Dead, we can be cured from ND00. I've labeled the vaccine "HS-18." It's found in the Book of Acts chapter one, verse 8.

Jesus said, "But you will receive power when the Holy Spirit comes on you; and you will be my witnesses in Jerusalem, and in all Judea and Samaria, and to the ends of the earth."

—Act 1:8

Inoculation is the placement of a serum or vaccine substance into the body that will grow or reproduce, boosting our immunity to a specific disease. The spiritual vaccine is found in the Holy Spirit. As believers, we have been inoculated with the power of the Holy Spirit.

Get Grafted

The reason we struggle in our walk of faith is because we rely on our own strength to propel us forward in our growth. Self-reliance equals failure.

Inoculate means "to graft a scion." A scion is the plant part to be grafted onto another plant. This is what Jesus was talking about in the parable of the Vine and Branches found in John:

I am the true vine, and my Father is the gardener. He cuts off every branch in me that bears no fruit, while every branch that does bear fruit he prunes[a] so that it will be even more fruitful. You are already clean because of the word I have spoken to you. Remain in me, as I also remain in you. No branch can bear fruit by itself; it must remain in the vine. Neither can you bear fruit unless you remain in me.

I am the vine; you are the branches. If you remain in me and I in you, you will bear much fruit; apart from me you can do nothing. If you do not remain in me, you are like a branch that is thrown away and withers; such branches are picked up, thrown into the fire and burned. If you remain in me and my words remain in you, ask whatever you wish, and it will be done for you. This is to my Father's glory, that you bear much fruit, showing yourselves to be my disciples.

—John 15:1-8

Fight the disease. Get your HS1-8 shot today. Then tell the rest of the world you found the cure for ND00.

A NOTE FROM ROB

Dear Reader,

I'm grateful that you chose this book, and I hope and pray you are able to use what you learned here to impact the young people in your community. Thank you for loving them and caring for them.

I've also written two youth devotionals you may find useful in your ministry. REGENER8 and ILLUMIN8 are available on Amazon.com. And keep an eye out for ACTVI8, to be released in 2018

Email your questions, comments, and success stories to me at rcook252underground@gmail.com. And be sure to check out my blog: www.regener8ted.com for more lesson materials.

ABOUT THE AUTHOR

Rob Cook lives in Philadelphia with his wife Stephanie, son
Christian, and several beloved pets.

www.ingramcontent.com/pod-product-compliance
Lightning Source LLC
Chambersburg PA
CBHW060207070426
42447CB00035B/2767